Future Ride

99 Ways the Self-Driving, Autonomous Car Will Change Everything from Buying Groceries to Teen Romance to Surviving a Hurricane to Turning Ten to Having a Heart Attack to Building a Dream Home to Simply Getting From Here to There

Version 2

by Peter Wayner

Contents

(◁ indicates a chapter that's only in version 2.)

As Wealthy as Scrooge McDuck

Imagine a world where everyone is rich, a world where everyone enjoys the trappings of wealth and the privileges that come along with it, a world where everyone lives a Scrooge McDuck life where the estates stretch for miles and swimming pools are filled with money.

"Impossible!" some will say. The economy runs on a winner-take-all rule and that rule holds true in all fields from surgery to steak houses. A few will be the best and they'll win the bulk of the money. There will always be a few that are wealthier than others. There can be only one Scrooge McDuck.

But what if wealth is not relative but absolute? What if the definition of wealthy is measured by the trappings themselves and not who has more of them? If so, the world is about to get much, much wealthier. Soon everyone will have access to one of the great movie clichés of the rich and powerful. Soon everyone will be able to snap their fingers and call for their chauffeur to bring their limousine around. Soon, we'll live in the world where everyone is able to relax as a chauffeur takes us where we want to go.

This is one way to look at the coming of the computer software that will drive a car from point A to point B. Computer scientists will talk about routing algorithms and machine vision software that can distinguish between a walking person and a lamppost. Physicists will talk about laser range finders and cameras. Lawyers will talk about liability. But everyone else will talk about the pleasure of having a chauffeur who will take them where they want to go.

Progress in the area has been incredibly rapid. The Defense Advanced Research Projects Agency (DARPA) sponsored their first "Grand Challenge" in 2004 along a 150 mile course in the middle of nowhere between California and Nevada. They asked university teams to build a car that could follow the road in the desert without a driver and the best car from Carnegie Mellon made it only 7.32 miles before it was stopped by a rock. A rock!

The next race in 2005 was very different. Five teams could finish the course and 22 made it farther than the 7.32 miles that the 2004 winner completed. Today the project isn't advanced enough for DARPA and the researchers have largely moved on to other projects.

Private corporations are working to bring all of this to the marketplace and they're experimenting with cars that either help in little ways or take over and do everything. Some are talking about small features that just help a human, like watching for someone in the way if you're trying to change lanes.

Others are aiming higher and they're so far along that people are only half-joking that the driverless car is literally just around the corner. If you live in California or Nevada, where the cars are now street legal, this may be true. Google has been talking publicly about their car which they say has gone hundreds of thousands of miles on the roads of California and Nevada without an accident. They aren't alone either.

Now car manufacturers are trying to leapfrog each other by sending their cars on longer and longer trips. Google's cars are commonplace in Silicon Valley. Mercedes sent their futuristic silver blob floating around San Francisco while discretely alerting the media and all of the Twitter users, bloggers and Redditors it could call.[223] Audi sent a car from San Francisco to Las Vegas. As I'm finishing this, Delphi announced plans to send their car on a 3,500 mile trip across America.[46] Sony has even announced their own movie comedy about autonomous cars.[170]

These cars will change everything. Sure the computer may drive like an old lady studying to pass the driver's license practical exam because it stops so firmly at each and every stop sign. Sure the algorithm may be impossibly earnest because it actually follows the speed limit as if it were a law of physics. But it will give everyone the freedom of billionaires to snap their fingers and call for a chauffeur.

Some of the changes will be obvious. People will have more time because they won't be driving a car. Everyone will be able to send text messages from the car because the computer will be watching the road.

Others aren't so obvious. The world will need fewer and fewer parking spots, upending the investment in parking garages and the vast paved fields around shopping malls. Pre-teenagers won't need to wait for a driver's license to escape from their parents' clutches. The self-driving cars may end up doing more than taking us from place to place, they might end up bringing a hot dinner and delivering medical care, too. Matt McFarland at the Washington Post noted that it's quite probable that the robot cars will save more lives than ending war, if only because many more people die on the highways each year than on the battlefield. [135]

What follows are 99 short chapters examining 99 different guesses about how our cities, our homes and our lives will change when cars drive themselves. Some are almost guaranteed to come to pass and others are just good guesses. Some will probably be wrong. Every part of our homes, our towns and our lives will be upended and it's hard to guess accurately about how all of the pieces will fit back together after the self-driving car smashes the world to bits.

What is clear, though, is that everyone will be much wealthier in absolute terms. We'll waste less time stuck in traffic, we'll burn less energy getting from A to B and we'll enjoy the capricious freedom that used to be the sole province of the people wealthy enough to employ a chauffeur. We'll all be able to snap our fingers like Scrooge McDuck and go where we want to be.

1

Cabs

Thomas Fairchild: I like to think of life as a limousine. Though we are all riding together, we must remember our places. There's a front seat and a back seat and a window in between.
Linus Larrabee: Fairchild, I never realized it before, but you're a terrible snob.
Thomas Fairchild: Yes, sir.

From "Sabrina"[250]

The model for the future car will be a taxi cab driven by a robot. When you want to go somewhere, you'll punch up an app on your mobile and book a car. These applications are already becoming common for reserving limousines and taxi cabs in many cities and their use will explode when autonomous cars appear. These fleets of reservable cars will dominate the roads and only the very rich or capricious will bother maintaining their own cars.

The autonomous cars will be able to price themselves lower than cabs because they won't have a driver. Assume a cab costs $30,000 and lasts two years. It requires two to three drivers during that time that make about $30,000 a year or more. The cost of the human can easily be 3 to 6 times the cost of the car.

Autonomous cars will also be able to offer cheaper rides and impromptu car pools with the automated scheduling software. (See chapter 4.) A rider could book an exclusive trip from door to door or allow the cab to match the rider up with other people going in the same direction. This will slow the trip and add detours but offer savings that

11

could be substantial. The scheduling algorithm will look for potential ride sharers and then split the fare as appropriate. The calculations could be complicated but this can be hidden from the rider. (See 44.) The mobile phone will just offer a list of options with various prices that shrink as more people are added to the car pool.

Some autonomous fleets will probably include larger vans and shuttle busses that will pick up larger groups along major routes. (See 24.) During the morning and evening rush hour, they'll move through the city like regular buses, offering discounts for people who meet the bus on street corners along major arteries. Routes will be designed and organized each day when the computers learn who will be traveling. There will be substantial discounts for non-refundable tickets because the algorithms will be able to plan the routes in advance to deliver the most people. There will also be discounts for those who are flexible enough to change their departure time to accommodate other riders.

The cabs will also automate the chatter that used to come from the human driver. The fleets of cabs are already opportunities for advertising (see 72) and this will only grow more sophisticated and immersive. If the advertising becomes lucrative enough, the cab rides may even be free to anyone who's willing to endure a pitch during the ride.

These ads and the computer software running the car will be communicating with the riders. They will serve up a mixture of facts (see 88) and suggestions (see 72), taking on the role that human cab drivers once provided. They may have encyclopedic knowledge that they download from some server but they'll never have the same character despite the best efforts of the computer scientists studying AI.

2

Multiple Cars

"My favorite Porsche is always the one I am just sitting in."

Jerry Seinfeld

The average car is forced to be a jack of all trades and a master of none. A big family is stuck with a van because they need one on the weekends, even if there are only one or two people in the van during the week. The contractor is stuck driving a pickup truck filled with expensive tools on Friday night. The commuter with an efficient small car can't take more than four people in the car on the weekends. Ownership is very restrictive.

Fleets of autonomous cars will free riders to choose the right vehicle for the trip. The fleets will be filled with trucks, vans, and fuel-sipping single-seaters. Fleet managers will be able to tune the cars to the needs of the local population and then price the rides according to demand. Rental companies like Zipcar already offer multiple choices including vans and pickup trucks. The fleets will do the same.

The variety will also range over the quality of the materials. Cheaper cars will offer basic seats that may be a bit worn. More expensive cars will come with leather and better electronics. People will be able to choose a fancy car for an expensive event and a basic car for getting to work.

Fleet owners will have much greater flexibility than current companies. Some cars for commuters will come with a desk. Others will come with a sink and mirror for primping. Some may offer horizontal beds for overnight trips. (See 76.) Cars for families or groups will have a central table for playing cards or eating the food that the car picks up at the restaurant along the way. It will be a rolling dining room, not a car.

The creative geniuses who build stretch limousines will bring their expertise to launch autonomous vans carrying pinball machines, hot tubs, bow hunting simulators, golf driving ranges, and maybe even something as boring as a reclining E-Z-Boy lounge chair with big screen television. Exercise bikes, rowing machines, and treadmills will be common. Weight lifting will probably be done with machines not free weights to avoid injury. If it's not too big, someone will find a way to stick it in a rolling van and rent rides to people who want to do something else while going to work.

3

Fuel Sippers

"Absolutely. This horsepower race is a bunch of b&%$ s%&, but you have to keep up with the Germans. We have to make a certain number of high horsepower cars because some people want them—and you magazine journalists like to write about horsepower—but I figure it's about over. I hope it is. Supercars have never been my deal; we need to go back to affordable performance. I like lighter cars that are fun to drive. I've always loved pocket-rockets.

"Back when I was building the Shelby cars for Chrysler," [Carroll Shelby] continued, "people said I was going to ruin my reputation by building smaller cars. Well, I don't give a s&*& - about my reputation; I just want to build cars that I like to drive. Cars like the V-6 Mustang. It's lighter and more fun to drive, and someone else will always have more horsepower."

From an interview with Carroll Shelby in "Road and Track"[53]

The curb weight of the low-end 2013 Honda Civic with automatic transmission is 2840 pounds, almost double the 1500 pounds of the original darling that appeared in 1973. No one should put on weight like that, but to be fair, the 2013 Civic is still one of the lighter cars on the market. Many of the SUVs and minivans easily exceed 4000 lbs and the 2013 Nissan Quest is more than 4500 pounds.

Accelerating all of this weight costs energy (and, to a much smaller extent, time). Fleets of autonomous vehicles can help the world break out of the economic model that forces them into bigger, heavier cars. Most commuters don't need to ride in a car that was built to hold four to seven people but they have no choice if they want a car that will hold everyone in their family at night or on weekends. They also don't need to ride to work in a car with a range of hundreds of miles before refueling. That's only necessary on long vacation trips. Yet the economic model of ownership forces people to buy the biggest car they'll need.

When riders stop buying complete cars and shift to purchasing them by the trip, the fleet owners can start matching cars to the trip and the rider. In some cases, this will mean large vans carrying a number of people downtown in the morning during rush hour, but in many cases it will mean one driver going to one destination in a car that can be very light. Fleet owners will be able to experiment with ultra light weight vehicles that consume much, much less energy to start and stop.

This can be taken to extremes for commuters. The basic model of the Segway, the i2, weighs only 105 pounds and the extreme version, the x2 Adventure, is not much heavier at 120 pounds. Either of these would make a good commuting vehicle for days with good weather. Adding a solid, wind-cheating shell and more batteries for multiple trips would probably double or triple the weight of these machines, but that would still make them very light. There are already several ultralightweight cars on the market that fit this vision. The Twike, from Germany, uses electric power to deliver the equivalent of more than 100 miles per gallon. The ELF from Organic Transit weigh only 150 pounds and the company claims they can get 1800 miles per gallon. [138]

There are hundreds of lightweight options like this on the drawing boards of dreamers who remember the days when a good Porsche was close to 2000 pounds. The fleet model of selling rides will unlock the possibilities as fleet owners can experiment with new models that offer very light weight transportation. Then they'll be able to pass on some of that energy savings to the user.

4

Car Pools

"When You Ride ALONE, You Ride with Hitler. Join a Car-Sharing Club TODAY!"

World War II Poster printed by the Government Printing Office for the Office of Price Administration [168]

The car pool was invented during World War II as a way to save gasoline for the battlefield and reborn during the 1970s when gasoline became hard to get again. Its popularity, if that's the right word, closely followed the availability of fuel and the car pools slowly disappeared when gas became cheap. They were largely pooling the liquid. The idea has taken on different forms and grown more ad hoc. In a process often called "slugging," passengers line up near bus stops and accept rides from drivers who need to carry more people to qualify for special lanes for cars with two or more riders. They are sharing access and the custom is often not to share the gas because the driver is gaining the chance to go faster in special lanes.

The arrival of fleets of autonomous cars will change that dynamic because the modern car pool will be designed to share the cost of hardware and fuel. Fleets will be able to group together people going in the same direction with much greater ease because they'll know where everyone is going. If there's a common destination, the computer algorithms can find it relatively easily. The centralized database makes it all possible.

The pooling can be very casual and ad hoc. The fleets can present each rider with a list of options that vary according to the length of the trip and the precision with which the car will deliver the rider to

17

the right place at the right time. The list can also offer discounts for riding with others and apply these discounts after the booking if the opportunity arises while the trip is in progress. A rider might agree to a price but ask the scheduler to look for people going in the same direction. If the trip can be split as the scheduler gets a request for someone along the route, the rider might get a discount of 40%. This would be optional, of course, and the rider could just reserve the car at full price and block any splitting.

When the lists of riders grows larger and some of the trips turn out to be common, the fleets may find that they have enough regular riders on some routes to have some choice in how the people are grouped together. The companies can start creating rolling clubhouses and matching people based on their interests. Ad hoc book clubs can be created, for instance, by matching people who've read the same books—information that could be gathered automatically from social media or the book sales companies.

Dating services may appear but it will depend upon how comfortable people feel sharing a vehicle with a stranger. Creating a feeling of security will be a general challenge for the autonomous companies but it's one that can be minimized with some surveillance. The cars will report their location constantly and they'll be directed by a central computer, largely eliminating the danger of being driven to some secluded location. There's a good chance the companies will require their customers to agree to constant video recording to discourage vandalism. This will also make riders feel more comfortable with each other.

The car designs may evolve to put passengers in separate compartments in the same vehicle, essentially putting barriers between the riders. This will may make people feel more secure, but it will also hurt the opportunity to talk and socialize. This seclusion, though, may be what riders largely choose. In "slugging", the riders follow a set of generally agreed upon rules including one of the most important: no talking unless the driver initiates the conversation.

5

Stress

"...if you put any group of mammals in a crowded situation, some sort of rage will occur. One of the people or one of the mice will be the first to break or snap or pop."

Jay Leno [125]

If Jean-Paul Sartre wasn't describing road rage when he wrote "No Exit," [187] he might as well have been. There's nothing more maddening than enduring the slights both small and large by the other drivers. "Hell is other drivers," he might have written.

Driving is exhausting because the stakes are so high and the rules of the road are so imperfect. What's the difference between changing lanes and cutting someone off? Just how long should one wait for the perfect moment to pull into traffic? There are no clear rules and that spurs anger and disputes. When the traffic is tight, our brains need to both navigate and make millions of decisions about the rules of the road. This turns commuting into a slow boil that often erupts into a dangerous rage.

Autonomous cars save us from much of that stress. They make decisions and save passengers the exhaustion that comes from thinking about what to do. The robots also depersonalize the experience. If another robot car cuts you off, it's because an algorithm decided to do it, not a human. Sure you can blame the programmers, but that team is a long way away, not in the car immediately in front of you.

There's no doubt the autonomous cars also strip away the fun of driving through mountain roads and enjoying the fun of piloting a well-oiled machine, but there are very few people who enjoy a daily commute like that. I know one couple who live on Skyline Drive, the road running along the ridge that forms the backbone of the San Francisco peninsula. They have a wonderful commute swerving through hairpin turns on their way down from the ridge. Then they hit the main roads and join the same traffic that the rest of us face.

Doctors routinely ask their patients whether there was traffic on the trip to the appointment. "I'm not just making small talk." wrote Dr. Arthur Agatson in *Prevention*. "Being stuck in traffic raises blood pressure and triples heart attack risk. So if a patient has had a tough commute and her BP is elevated, I'll recheck it later."[89]

One study claimed that road rage produced 218 murders and 12,000 injuries during the 1990s.[89] Another in the New England Journal of Medicine found that exposure to traffic increased the odds of a myocardial infarction by 2.92 times.[63;159] There are countless others that connect the stress of driving a car to death. One study in Sweden showed that women were affected more than men by the grind of a long commute.[221]

The New England Journal of Medicine study did not distinguish between the people who experience traffic as a driver and those who are passengers on public transportation. Autonomous cars won't save us from some of the frustration of being delayed in traffic and chaos—although the autonomous vehicles should reroute us more efficiently—but they will let us distract ourselves with electronic gadgets, reading and other fun. We won't need to sit idling behind the wheel waiting to inch forward through a traffic jam, one of the most aggravating chores I've endured.

Trips in an autonomous car will be more like sitting in the living room or, perhaps, a massage therapist's chair. The stress of navigating, steering, dodging, and maneuvering will be replaced by a question like, "What color nail polish should I put on?" If something does go wrong and traffic appears, it only means more time in the easy chair getting a massage or enjoying the ride.

6

Capital Costs

BB Now don't try to hustle me here ... you know what I mean. I hate being hustled. Give me an honest price, not one of your 'special' deals... give me an honest price. Do I make myself clear?

SALESMAN Now, how much are you willing to pay?

BB There ya go... there ya go... you're doing it... you're doing one of those hustle numbers.

SALESMAN I'm just trying to get an idea how much you're willing to pay.

BB Four dollars... I want to pay four dollars a month.

SALESMAN That's not an honest answer.

BB What do ya want to hear? That I'd love to pay three hundred and fifty a month... is that what you want to hear? Tell me how much you want me to pay and I'll tell you how much I'll pay, but don't do a hustle on me... I don't like that. How much do I want to pay? I'd like to pay nothing!

From "Tin Men" [127]

One of my neighbors used to use her car once each week to drive to the supermarket. Then, she started getting the food delivered and she rarely drove at all. While she is an extreme case, even the cars of the heaviest commuters are parked 20 hours a day. The average car is said to be parked 23 hours or so.

All of this sitting around is a waste. Many of the cars rust or fall apart long before their moving parts fail from the stress of actually rolling. The rubber components dry out, the steel rusts, and the paint slowly decomposes under the relentless power of the sun. Many of the breakdowns on a car are caused by use, but many are caused by the passage of time. (See 23.)

The cars are also financially rusting. The new car that costs $30,000 is tying up that money that could be in the bank. Not only is the car depreciating in value, but the capital is not earning interest. If the owner takes out a loan, the car loan could be 3%, 4% or higher depending upon the interest rates at the time. This cost of capital is significant. A car that lasts 15 years will cost 42% more in either car payments or lost interest assuming a rate of 5%.

There's one class of car that isn't always sitting around letting the capital value rust away: taxis. A good cab company keeps its cars rolling as much as possible. The best ones keep the same car rolling through two 12-hour shifts a day; something that's possible in big cities like New York where there's always someone looking for a ride some-where. Autonomous vehicles run by automated cab companies will bring this same discipline to the average home car. They may never stay on the road for 24 hours each day, especially in the bedroom communities where people keep regular hours, but they will be able to save fortunes by reducing the capital cost of riding in a car.

Autonomous vehicles will wear out sooner, but they will travel many more miles. A good school bus can easily go several million miles. A PBS documentary of the taxi business in New York estimated that the average cab covers 360 miles in a day.[256] That's more than 120,000 miles in a year. In two years, the average taxi will travel farther than even the best private cars do in the 20-30 years that they can stay on the road.

These taxis dramatically reduce the capital cost because they roll all day long. A cab that packs the same mileage into two years instead of 15 only requires a capital cost of 5.2% instead of 42%. That's a big savings that could, in some way, eventually be passed along to the customer.

7

Prices

"A dog has no use for fancy cars, big homes, or designer clothes. A
water-logged stick will do just fine."

"Marley & Me" [72]

Will autonomous cars be cheaper over the long run? Or will they
just have extra features that drive up the cost? The price tag for a new
car is one number but it pays for a big collection of parts and features,
some expensive and some cheap. The proportions of the budget given
to these extras will change dramatically as some features disappear and
others will get fancier. Some of this will be invisible to the people who
choose to buy each ride individually but the few people who choose to
continue to buy cars will notice the shift in prices. Who will win? It's
hard to guess at the final change, but it's possible to identify the forces
and guess.

The biggest change will be in the number of vehicles made
each year. If the number of miles driven each year remains the
same—something that's not guaranteed if people start thinking about
the cost (see 47)—then the number of cars needed could drop. If each
car is used ten hours a day instead of one thanks to good scheduling
algorithms, then we may need one tenth the number of cars. The real
drop could be more if people share rides or less if people take more
rides. (See 80.)

The problem is that many of the fixed costs for producing a car,
such as design costs, will remain the same but will be split between
far fewer car buyers. This will almost certainly push up prices perhaps

even dramatically. Someone who wants to actually buy a car won't be able to share the development costs with as many people.

But this effect may not be as dramatic if the marketplace makes fewer car designs and spends less on car designers. If the manufacturers reduce the number of designs and limit the amount of effort that goes into making each new car look cool, the development costs can be much smaller and spread over the same number of people.

The amount of chrome and eye-catching curves on the car will probably decrease when people have less emotional investment in their cars (see 83, 41 and 39). This will simplify the creation process and lower the fixed costs.

The big sales teams focused on making one big ticket sale every seven to ten years will disappear but this won't necessarily lead to a cheaper bottom line. They'll only be replaced by a marketing team designed to keep people coming back to the same cab company again and that will mean the massive continual brand advertising will continue in a different form because their customers make a new decision each day. The autonomous cab companies will probably follow their lead and also emulate the frequent flyer programs run by the airlines.

The car designers may be able to shave dollars off the prices when they cut the weight of the cars. (See 25.) If the cars are safe enough to reduce the need for steel cages and protective equipment, they can also get cheaper when these are left off of the cost.

The cost of maintenance and upkeep will also shift. The autonomous owners will be able to take advantage of all of the economies of scale that go with hiring in-house mechanics to run large fleets. Getting rid of the billing overhead and centralizing part purchase will drive down the costs. This will be balanced by the higher price of maintaining things that are not owned by the users. People never take as good care of hotel rooms or rental cars and this capricious attitude is eventually passed along to the customer in higher replacement costs.

Which of these effects will win? It's impossible to guess because the business will shift so much, but it's likely that the cost of actually buying a car will rise. Fewer people in the market will leave car ownership as a hobby for rich people with the time and energy to invest in the machines. Just as private airplanes have gotten more and more expensive over time, private car ownership will probably follow.

8

Maintenance

For the first seventy or so years of their existence, cars came with
the job of taking care of them. The average car owner learned to worry
about changing the oil, rotating the tires, flushing the coolant system
and other tasks. Many of the more mechanically talented car owners spent their Saturdays under the hood, fiddling with the engine and
keeping them running. Maintenance was just something that car owners needed to worry about.

That job has been getting harder and harder for shade tree mechanics to handle. The space under the hood is so jammed that it's often
hard to replace the spark plugs, a job that used to take ten minutes.
When the computer systems work, they tune the car better than any
human could ever do. When they don't work, they're impossible to fix.
Cars are becoming black boxes.

Maintenance for privately owned cars is becoming harder to do
and that makes it more expensive. The manufacturers compete to offer
good warranties, but when the warranties expire, there's no incentive
to make it easy to care for the cars. Plastic parts that probably cost
pennies to make are resold through the dealers for $20, $30 or more.
Sophisticated parts are thousands of dollars. One friend of mine drove
a new car into a deep puddle and shorted out the computer. The in-

surance company took one look and wrote off the car. It was a total loss. Fixing it would cost more than the $20,000+ the car would cost to replace.

Owners of fleets of autonomous cars have different incentives. They can hire teams of mechanics who aren't billing by the hour or by the job. The owners and the mechanics just want keep the cars rolling and out of their shop. The fleets will probably use many cars of the same model allowing them to purchase the replacement parts at reasonable prices. The mechanics will learn the idiosyncrasies of these cars and fix them faster.

The manufacturers will also have different incentives. If they sell to the fleets—or if they run the fleets themselves—they'll want to design the cars for simple maintenance. If the spark plugs are hard to replace, the designers will hear about it. To be fair, my car came with plugs that only need to be replaced only every 100,000 miles, so the manufacturers are moving in that direction

The engines themselves may just be cartridges that are easy to replace. It's easy to imagine a hybrid gas/electric car that gets its electricity from one of those portable, gas-powered generators normally sold for emergencies. When the engine fails, a swap only takes two minutes.

Streamlining the maintenance like this will let us squeeze more life out of the cars. While the currently available cars are much more reliable than the cars from the 1970s, the cost of maintenance is still too high. If new cars are being crushed just because some water flooded the computer chamber, there's plenty of good hardware on the car that's going to waste.

All it takes is one look at a 20-year-old car to recognize what can last. The chassis, glass, suspension system and exterior body could easily last 50 to 60 years with just a small amount of maintenance. Even the drive-train full of moving parts could routinely live for 30-40 years with a regular shot of grease. Some engine parts like the piston rings wouldn't last much longer than they do today, but the engines could be rebuilt as they often are today.

There will be challenges because fleet-owned rental cars aren't treated as well as cars driven by their owners. The chairs, door handles, and other parts touched by humans would need to be replaced more frequently, but that could be made simpler with better design. The system could also track down the worst offenders who vandalize the cars because the next rider will report any damage to avoid the blame.

The autonomous cars won't suffer the same mistreatment from drivers as rental cars, though, because the car will answer to the owner. It won't go too fast, turn too quickly or stress the car because it won't be programmed to do it.

A fleet of autonomous vehicles will be able to extend the life of all of these parts, driving down the cost of the cars by squeezing a longer life out of them.

9

Paying for Roads

Cop Hey, you think you own the whole road?
Mr. Wheeler Hmph! Of course I own the road. My taxes pay for them. I voted for road bonds. I pay for the roads and I'll use 'em.

From "Motor Mania"[118]

At the beginning of 2013, the Oregon legislature turned to confront a new scourge: very efficient cars that consume less gas to go farther. Normally, the politicians would be cheering something so obviously green and good for the carbon footprint of the state, but this day they were worried about their roads. The efficient cars were being blamed for a big gap in the road construction budget financed by gas taxes.[237;254]

The rise of autonomous cars has the opportunity to change how we pay for roads. In the beginning, it may be simplest to leave the gasoline tax in place because there will still be legacy vehicles on the road, but when the autonomous cars become dominant, the flood of new information may make it easier to move to a mileage tax. The Oregon legislators imagine an electronic tracking device that will record each and every mile like a taxicab meter. You'll pay up each month for the meter. They've already tested a program where the meter replaced the gas tax.

There are already a number of places where people pay a mileage fee for the roads. Most highway tolls are calculated based on how many miles you move along the road. Longer trips usually mean longer tolls. The meters will push this system to local roads, too.

Some of the newest toll roads change their prices during the day depending upon demand. A more advanced system will change the price of driving on a road based upon time and date. The cars will be bidding for reservations to drive on the road at a particular time and this will be passed along to the riders when they book a car ride.

A reservation system like this will shift the cost of maintaining the roads to the wealthiest people who choose to drive at peak times. Others will be able to save money by traveling at off hours or by limiting their travels altogether. The only downside is that the current gas tax acted like a carbon tax by rewarding the most efficient cars and that subsidy will disappear. Of course, the reservation system for taxing travel could be adjusted to give a credit to carbon-neutral cars or cars that somehow helped the community in other ways, perhaps by offering free rides to the poorest.

A sophisticated reservation system will create more pressure on rural regions where few people drive long roads that cost a similar amount to maintain per mile as the heavily trafficked city streets. Heavy traffic can put much more wear than occasional cars but the cost per passenger mile will almost certainly be much lower in the city. It won't take long for someone to compile the data and discover just how much more expensive it is to maintain roads in the countryside. Will the city dwellers revolt and use the power of their votes to cut back on maintenance of country roads? Will many of the country roads disappear altogether? Or will only the rich be able to afford to live in the middle of nowhere?

Paying for Everything◁

Cop
Mr. Wheeler Hmph!

From "Motor Mania" [118]

Paying for roads by taxing fleets of autonomous cars is an obvious solution to reforming the current gasoline tax-based system, which has suffered as cars become more fuel efficient and motorists drive fewer miles. Cities will be able to use revenue from fleet rentals to build pathways that are most desirable. (See 9.) An interesting question is whether they should also use these fees to support other services. Could transportation taxes become the dominant way to fund government?

This isn't so far-fetched. While gas taxes and tolls on bridges are often said to simply pay for the roads or the bridges, they often generate surpluses that support the general fund. Revenues from tolls on bridges and tunnels going into Manhattan, for example, pay for other city services that support the excitement that attracts travelers. The high cost of the Lincoln tunnel is, in essence, a tax that pays for the city that never sleeps that Frank Sinatra sang about in the theme song for the movie, "New York, New York." [73;173]

There are some advantages to using surpluses from cab fleet taxes to pay for schools, firetrucks and more. Moving about the city is a basic need used by all members of society and it's closely tied to economic activity. Those taxes will fall broadly on many shoulders and they will fall hardest on those who are drawing a salary. Taxes could be timed to be higher at rush hour to nab commuters. The young, the old, the unemployed and the infirm tend to travel less and so they would bear less of the burden.

However, taxing movement discourages movement and that means fewer visits and more long nights at home with the tube. Do we really want to tax the interaction with each other, one of the joys of being alive?

11

Stop Lights

This paper analyses the results from the Cabstand junction in Portishead, near Bristol, which failed for a few hours in June 2009 and has since been the site of a ground-breaking experiment to remove all junction controls. The Cabstand trial, still ongoing over a year later, has been followed by a further two trials in Bristol and the results from these trials are analysed. Although it is acknowledged that further research is needed nevertheless the trials demonstrated that despite their differences the junctions generally performed better without traffic signal or any formal control.

Keith Firth [65]

Every driver knows that pleasure that comes from seeing a red light in the distance and then slowing down the right amount to reach the intersection just after the light turns green again. There's no need to stop or accelerate, no need to tap your fingers on the steering wheel waiting for the light to change. If only all of interactions in life could be synchronized so gracefully.

They can be in the world of autonomous vehicles. Stop lights are primitive beacons that communicate only with sighted humans. They reach people only in a clear line of sight. The next generation can broadcast the green signals with a radio beacon that reaches around corners. An even better version can post the green light schedule on some kind of web site so every car can look up the green moments and plan the schedule in advance. Planning the right speed isn't hard. Any high school kid can do the math by dividing the distance to the corner by the amount of time until the next green light. It's just division.

The Internet beacons broadcasting the green light schedules for safely entering an intersection don't need to be limited to corners that currently have stop lights. All intersections can have a schedule, even the ones that don't merit a stop sign today. The number is small enough to be bundled into a manageable file. To see this, imagine that there is one intersection for every 100 residents. Then imagine that the schedule for each can be encoded in 100 bytes. That's 300MB for the United States.

In practice, the schedule for an intersection can probably be reduced to just a few bits on average by setting standard schedules and assigning most of the corners to one of a few standards. The north and southbound cars, for instance, might be clear to go for the first 20 seconds of each minute while the east and westbound cars would be free to travel on the second block of 20 seconds. Cars turning north or south could get a ten second block and the cars turning east or west would get the last ten second block. Then it would repeat.

When the green light listings become common, the system can be made even more efficient and even a bit safer by speeding it up. Faster? This sounds counter-intuitive because slower cars are usually safer cars when humans are driving, but the computers are fast enough so they can handle split-second decisions just as easily at 200 mph as 40 mph. Faster cars are safer cars, at least at corners, because they block the intersection for less time. The faster a car zips through the intersection, the less time it spends in the intersection where it's available to crash into another. [1]

When everything speeds up, the slices of time allocated to each direction at the corner can be cut shorter and shorter. It's conceivable that the length of a green light could be cut to half a second, reducing the amount of adjustment that each car will need to make coming into an intersection.

Automated stop light beacons like this will have dramatic effects on the efficiency of the transportation network. Much of the energy used by cars is wasted and turned into heat when cars slow down and then accelerate. While regenerative braking can capture some of this loss, it's still a significant waste because batteries can't absorb all of the energy as quickly as possible. Some estimates suggest that regen-

---

[1] This claim about safety only applies to the danger of crashing. A faster car carries more kinetic energy and that energy has to go some where in a crash. That makes them more dangerous.

erative brakes recapture 20% of the energy at the cost of a significant amount of complexity for the vehicles.[28]

The cars that don't stop also don't waste energy idling at the lights. Some systems that turn off the engines when the cars are idling at a stoplight are can save 15% of the energy used during average city driving, at least according to one estimate from Discovery Channel.[155] The autonomous vehicles that cruise through stop lights won't need to shut down their engines at lights saving the energy without the complexity of trying to guess when to stop and restart the engine.

The greatest gift, though, will be making trips shorter. It's easy to imagine that some city trips are twice as long as they might be without stoplights. Simply precomputing the right speed between intersections to avoid stop lights could cut the travel time in half by eliminating all of that poky time spent waiting for the stopped cars to get up to speed again.

The gains could be even greater if the autonomous vehicles are precise enough to increase the speed limit in the cities. The only real limitation to going 80 to 100 miles per hour in the city streets is handling the tight turns without rolling over. Straight trips could easily average well over 100mph. Suddenly there wouldn't be a need for the kind of elevated freeways with limited access designed just so human drivers can maintain a decent speed. Every street could be like a freeway.

This may not be practical, though, if humans are crossing the streets or drifting into traffic. Jaywalking becomes much more dangerous when the cars appear so quickly that you don't have time to get out of the way. And then there will be those people who still want to drive their own cars but won't be able to match the precision of the automated machines.

12

Lanes

"The story of what happens one day in New York when a young lawyer and a businessman share a small automobile accident on F.D.R. Drive and their mutual road rage escalates into a feud."

Plot summary of "Changing Lanes"[219]

In one episode of "Seinfeld", Cosmo Kramer adopts a section of a highway and repaints the four lanes to be what he calls a "two lane comfort cruise." The extra wide lanes are supposed to be easier for drivers to navigate and more enjoyable for everyone. In the future, every stretch of road will get the Kramer treatment and everyone will be able to choose the width of their path through life.[149]

Autonomous cars will redefine lanes by opening up the opportunities for the computer reservation system to redraw them again and again and again. Wide cars can get a swath that's 12 feet wide while a motorcycle might be allocated just 3 feet. The computer drivers will be more precise making it possible to get rid of the normal padding and pack more cars into the same width. A four lane road might handle five or six cars across or more if people are traveling in thin commuter cars that may dominate rush hours. (See 2.)

This feature will also allow really wide loads that are two or three times as wide as conventional wide trucks. It will be possible to move entire homes from factories instead of building them on site. (See 92.) Manufacturers will be able to book two or three conventional lanes to move items that are just too big to ship today.

A good reservation system will also be able to change the direction of roads according to demand. Many cities already change the direc-

tion of lanes between the morning and evening rush hour. A sophisticated reservation system can change them more frequently to adapt to
special events like ball games or street fairs.

This flexibility will be countered by the desire to reduce the amount
of paving. (See 33.) If the roads shrink to be two, thin parallel paths
like railroads, they will save paving and introduce more green space
to neighborhoods, but they won't offer the same amount of flexibility. Shippers will need to reserve one, two or three lanes instead of
reserving by the foot.

13

Topology

"Sam must find a way to find his father and escape the Grid while also learning the dangers of having a destructive attitude."

Plot summary of the movie "Tron" [21]

The early city designers quickly settled on a grid as the most efficient way to split up the land between transportation and living. The grid in Manhattan is so all encompassing that architectural historians devote themselves to studying the form. [10] Hannah Higgins traces the development of the grid from the Old Kingdoms of Egypt (2695-2160 B.C.) through Greece, Rome, and modern Manhattan in *The Grid Book*. [94] She writes, "In the Babylonian creation myth, God turned men out like bricks from clay molds. It was men who built bricks into walls. The first grid, the brick wall, easily evokes associations with the human body."

The invention of the car changed the city grids. Too many people wanted to go faster than the city grid with its stoplights could support. Most of the city planners tried to fix this problem by adding big highways that were often elevated. Chicago built three big expressways radiating from the center. New York wrapped the island with highways so people could move north and south at 60+ m.p.h. Los Angeles was built around the freeways that came first, before the buildings built alongside.

Autonomous cars will change the city grid again making it new by eliminating the need for stop lights. (See 11.) Good routing algorithms and well-timed cars should be able to move through the city grid without stopping at corners. Just as cities already time the stop lights to speed travel on the major arteries, good algorithms will make it possible for people to move around the grid at fast speeds without stopping. Will autonomous cars travel at freeway speeds? It may be too dangerous at first for pedestrians but it may be possible when the walkers grow accustomed to cars blasting through the neighborhoods.

Will the freeways that act like arteries survive? The older freeways will probably hang on for some time because they are simpler to use for everyone including the autonomous cars. Everyone will be able to go faster on the freeways and that may justify keeping them around for a bit. Eventually, though, they will probably fall prey to their high costs. Some cities are already removing the elevated freeways. San Francisco trashed the elevated road along the Embarcadero after an earthquake weakened it—and discovered that traffic could flow nicely along the street level with properly timed street lights. When autonomous cars zip through intersections without stopping, more cities will probably follow this path because elevated freeways can be so expensive. Boston's Big Dig cost almost $15 billion, a cost of about $1 billion per mile. [124]

A deeper question for designers will be whether the grid makes the most sense. Most cities are stuck with their current layout—for now—but it may become economically possible to roll up large blocks of land and redevelop them. Some cities like Detroit are so poor that they are condemning land and returning it to countryside. [15;132] A similar project could drive urban redevelopment to morph into a new form.

Does another topology offer any advantage? Paris is designed around hubs and spokes that link so-called squares and railroad stations. The plots of land won't be rectangular adding many odd corners to the buildings built on top of this new design. Some people will love the idea of anything that isn't as regular as a grid. The good news is that autonomous cars should be able to handle all of them with the same aplomb—if an algorithm could be imagined as driving like some sports car fanatic as it guides the car through the roundabouts at the hubs. The autonomous cars should handle roundabouts better than humans and speed through them like intersections.

14

Energy Costs

"Energy expenditure and quality of life are the same thing. Things that make your energy expenditure go up make you feel good. Like ephedrine, it's off the market. Coffee—for two hours, but then you need another hit like me. Things that make your energy expenditure go down like starvation or hypothyroidism make you feel lousy. How many calories you burn and how good you feel are synonymous."

Robert Lustig[131]

The web site `hypermiling.com` is devoted to squeezing every last mile out of a tank of gas with techniques like accelerating slowly and tempering your competitive edge to fit in with the flow of traffic. The most obsessive devotees crawl up hills, ease away from stoplights and coast as much as possible, enabling them to double or even triple the official EPA estimate for their car.

Many of the techniques are a bit difficult to embrace because they are almost embarrassingly different from the way that people normally drive. Hypermilers often poke along because gunning the engine wastes fuel. Most people get competitive behind the wheel and that ruins fuel economy.

Autonomous cars, though, don't care whether they beat the car next to them off the line. They don't feel the need to race up the hills, unless their programmer tells them to go as fast as possible. All of the techniques used by hypermilers can be adapted for autonomous vehicles. In many cases, the autonomous car can do a better job than the human because the car has so much more knowledge.

A smart route planner, for instance, will know where the hills and valleys will slow down and speed up the car. The software can calculate the absolute minimum amount of fuel to dump into the cylinders so the car will barely crest the top of the hill before coasting down the hill and recapturing all of that energy. The software knows when an extra drop of fuel is wasted and when it's necessary to get the car through the next traffic light.

Smart cars can also adopt techniques that are hard for humans to pull off. Some hypermilers speak of *platooning*, a technique where the cars form a long chain through tailgating. Overcoming wind resistance is one of the biggest energy costs and a car that rides directly behind another doesn't need to burn as much fuel to slice through the air. Bike racers instinctively draft behind each other to save their strength and cars can similarly draft to improve fuel efficiency.

One episode of "Mythbusters" explored the topic and found that cars that follow 10 feet behind a big truck can cut their fuel use by 39%.[100] They tried driving the car only two feet behind and found that the car used more gas. It's a fine challenge for optimization that even the most obsessive human hypermiler would have trouble doing regularly.

Autonomous vehicles driven by computers excel at simply following a few feet behind a leader. A well-designed drafting program should be able to routinely save cars 30% to 40% with just basic programming and platooning.

A well-run system can also incorporate platooning into trip scheduling. If riders accept a bit of variability in arrival time, routing software can group together cars, buses and trucks sharing the same path. Higher fuel costs for the first in line can be shared by everyone behind. If one of the cars is much bigger, it can take the lead and earn a bonus for this sacrifice.

15

Teen Drivers

"Les, that license in your wallet, that's not an ordinary piece of paper. That is a driver's license, and it's not only a driver's license, it's an automobile license, and it's not only an automobile license, it's a license to live, a license to be free, a license to go wherever, whenever and with whomever you choose."

Corey Feldman in "License to Drive" [222]

Aside from perhaps the telephone, there may be no invention more closely aligned with teenage culture than the car. Movies like "Rebel Without a Cause" and "American Graffiti" cemented the connection between cars and the freedom to roam. When the nature of the car changes, so will teenage culture.

The biggest practical change will be driving safety because teenagers have dramatically higher accident rates. They are naturally impetuous and invincible, two bad traits for drivers. Some have tried to combat this by forcing teenagers to wait until they're 17 or 18 to get a license, but this may only delay the kind of crashes that come from inexperience. [30;76]

Scott Masten, a researcher for the California Department of Motor Vehicles, studied accident records and found that tougher laws did cut back on crashes caused by 16 year olds. But this didn't solve the problem.

"When you look at the bigger picture across 18- and 19-year-olds, it looks like we're offsetting those saved crashes," Masten told Anahad O'Connor at the *New York Times*, "In fact, 75 percent of the fatal crashes we thought we were saving actually just occurred two years later. It's shocking."[148]

Autonomous vehicles will eliminate this danger.

Teen passengers will be just as safe as law-abiding, middle-aged riders—- at least as long as they don't do something else while riding. One father told me in all earnestness that this may just make things worse for fathers because in the past at least one youngster's hands were occupied by the steering wheel.

Many of the classic dangerous pranks are made a bit easier by autonomous cars. Now everyone in the car can be mooning people, throwing rotten eggs, tossing toilet paper or displaying the manicure on their middle fingers. Whoever was driving will now have idle hands.

But they will be more closely watched.

Cars will keep scrupulous records of where they go and probably will report this back to the person paying the bills. Parents will know where their kids went and with whom they rode.

Teen drunk driving will also be a thing of the past, although more responsible teens won't have a reason to stay sober.

And scheduled cars will also remove any spontaneity. (See 47.) Kids will be less likely to go cruising, aimlessly looking for a good time or a party because the cars will be booked in advance. Renting out the car for four or five hours on a Friday night will be dramatically more expensive than just booking it for a ride to a party and back. All of the romance that dominated "American Graffiti" will be gone.

The good news is that the teenagers will be given a chance to reimagine their lifestyles and choose something distinct from their parents. They'll be able to tell their parents in all seriousness that it really is different now—and they'll be right.

16

Pre-Teen Drivers

"Sgt. Jerry Parker added that the little girl, who is not being iden-
tified, is tall for her age[, 6,] and also added 'how she knew how to
operate a car, your guess is as good as mine.'
The little joy-rider hit 2 parked cars on her journey and pushed one of
those parked cars into a third vehicle. The car and driver eventually
stopped after striking a utility pole."[246]

Richard Webster reporting in *The Examiner*

Before they are old enough to get a driver's license, children are
held in orbit around their parents. If they want to go somewhere, parents must take them. They're captive because they aren't old enough
to legally operate a car.

Self-driving cars will also change all of that. If kids are old enough
to be alone, they're old enough to ride in a driverless car. How young is
that? Parents in Japan let their 6-year-olds travel on the subway alone.
Many parents in America routinely leave their kids alone when they're
10 or 11. Some states even have laws that draw a bright line establish-
ing when kids are old enough to take care of themselves. Driverless
cars will give them access to the world.

Some parents will be overjoyed by this freedom. If the kids need
to go to soccer practice, mom or dad won't need to drive. If the kids
need to go to the library to work on a paper, the kids can just book a
ride like a grownup. (See 46.)

Other parents will be worried and threatened. It's scary enough for
some parents to let 16-year-olds drive anywhere in town; it's another to
let 12-year-olds or even 9-year-olds go wherever they want whenever

they want.

Automated cab companies will probably develop parental controls allowing parents to keep a tight leash on their kids. Children may have the ability to book a ride, but only if the person with the credit card approves. There will probably be a list of pre-approved destinations but everything else will need to be booked by the parents.

Cabs will probably also be able to broadcast video so parents can watch their kids, who will grow up with constant surveillance even when their parents are halfway around the world. In that sense, they'll never be alone.

17

Older Drivers

"For the study, which appeared in the Journal of the American Geriatrics Society, Rolison and his colleagues reviewed UK police records on all fatal road accidents reported between 1989 and 2009. They found that the risk of dying behind the wheel was similar for older adult drivers and young people every time they got in the car. Thirteen in 100 million driving trips ended in fatality among those under 29 years of age, compared to 14 in 100 million trips for people over 70."

Reuters [177]

Traffic accidents plague the young and the old alike. Younger drivers often misjudge obstacles in front of them and get in head-on collisions while older drivers don't judge distances as well and end up getting hit on the side when they pull out into traffic too late. While younger drivers are inexperienced, older drivers are haunted by deteriorating vision and reflexes, particularly at night and in bad weather. Although statistics show older drivers are getting better, the over 65 age group was once second only to 16- to 20-year-olds, but they have been passed by 21- to 34-year olds. [1]

Autonomous vehicles will change all of this for older drivers who will be able to travel to the store, the park, the theater or wherever they want to go. They won't need to wait for a bus or go to wherever the minibus from the assisted living facility is going that day. They will be driven wherever they want, when they want, often at a lower rate because they are more likely to travel during off hours. Long walks from the parking lot also will no longer be an issue because autonomous cars will pull right up to the door of the theater, mall or supermarket.

47

The biggest winners will be the people who enjoy living at their own suburban home but can't see well enough to drive. They are usually forced to move to some sort of assisted living apartment long before they need it, simply because they can't handle the driving it takes to maintain a home and buy food. The autonomous vehicle will change how people live as they grow older, making it more possible to age in place.

Self-driving vehicles may also unlock different social opportunities. They can act as a rolling adult day care center, looping through the neighborhoods to collect a circle of friends before heading off to an event. They may even have built in bridge or mahjong tables for longer trips.

There will be challenges. Most of the options for the elderly today are driven by humans who also help the people in and out of the car. They may carry heavier packages and help the passengers negotiate stairs and icy walks. Autonomous cars won't be able to do any of this. While the next generation of designs will almost certainly produce small buses that are easy for everyone to board, the computer can't help with heavy things and tricky sidewalks. The cars will also be of limited help in more rural areas although they might generate enough demand to spur the design of autonomous Jeeps and all terrain vehicles. These might do more than help us get around as we get older, they might actually make life better than it was before.

18

Handicapped Travel

A blind person can drive a car safely by following instructions given by a passenger.—CONFIRMED Adam and Jamie first tried driving while blindfolded but failed miserably. When a truly blind person was behind the wheel, he could drive fairly well. Adam and Jamie also tested the circumstance of the passenger (instructor) being intoxicated. This caused communication to break down and resulted in erratic, dangerous driving, much like the driver himself was drunk. Finally, the MythBusters speculated that a person rendered blind before they could get a driver's license would lack preconceptions about driving, making following instructions less difficult than if they had previous driving experience.

Summary of Mythbusters research on blind drivers [102]

Getting from point A to point B isn't as simple for many people and that's why handicapped parking spots were invented. The door-to-door service provided by the autonomous cars will change the game for many handicapped people and give them more equal access to the world. Many handicapped won't need parking spots or accommodations because the average vehicles will serve their needs and drop them at the front door, closer than ever.

The blind will be some of the biggest winners because they will be able to book rides from the same fleets as the sighted. Both will request the car with their voice avoiding the need for anyone to use their eyes. [181]

This will change the economics of being handicapped. Everything gets cheaper when the business is able to serve a wider population. Many of the handicapped won't need to spend extra for customized cars or human drivers. They'll get the same rates as everyone else.

There will still need to be some cars for people who can't use a cane to walk to the curb. There will probably be cars that let wheelchairs roll right up into them. These won't have the same low average costs but the riders will still enjoy the benefits of letting the autonomous car handle the driving. Some of these specialized vehicles will end up being like light ambulances offering basic medical services. Rolling dialysis clinics might let those with kidney failure clean their blood while traveling.

Even average users might choose these light duty ambulances occasionally. Commuters might request one of these medical vans once a month to get a checkup and watch their medical statistics, all while going to work.

19

Differently Abled

> "A group of wheelchair-bound individuals decide that it is time to get even when an inconsiderate, non-handicapped man uses the handicapped-designated parking area and bathroom stall in a public building. This light-hearted comedy sends a message of respect and awareness for the rights of disabled persons."

Synopsis of "Handicapped". [51]

The blind and the old may be some of the most obvious beneficiaries from robot cars (see 18 and 17) but there a number of other people who may not be officially handicapped but still have trouble driving cars. Some of the people on the spectrum of autism or with other birth disorders like Downs Syndrome may have perfectly good eyes and ears but they're not ready for the complexity of navigating the roads. Some adults that may not even fall into these categories are still unable to manage all of the simultaneous responsibilities of driving a car. Autonomous cars will liberate them all.

The most obvious beneficiaries will be those who can handle jobs. The self-driving cars will be able to take them to and from their work at the same cost as the average human. There won't be any need for a driver and a special van, something that often limits economic competitiveness.

The cars can also offer a certain amount of surveillance and light supervision for those that need it. Remote teams that watch over large groups with cameras and interactive video chat. Reducing the need for extra help can make the labor more cost competitive.

Many advocates for people who fall into these categories work hard to find good, honest jobs because they understand that having a role and a purpose in the economy is an important part of an individual's self-respect. When the robot cars can make it possible for more people to travel as needed, more people can take real roles in society.

20

Pedestrians

Rachael May I ask you a personal question?
Deckard Sure.
Rachael Have you ever retired a human by mistake?
Deckard No.
Rachael But in your position, that is a risk.

From "Bladerunner"[59]

Roads may be built for cars but humans walk across them from time to time and this can be dangerous. The National Highway Traffic Safety Administration counted 4,280 pedestrian deaths and more than 70,000 injuries in 2010. All involved human drivers.[69;151]

Could robots be worse? Computers crash often enough that many will be wary. My printer, for instance, gets confused and refuses to do anything at least once a month. Even if robot cars are ten times more reliable than our ink-jet printers, that could end up being terrible for pedestrians.

We won't know until we do the experiment on a large scale, but the early results from Google and the various DARPA challenges are promising. Computers are apparently more trustworthy than humans, especially multi-tasking humans racing to send text messages while rushing to daycare to pick up the kid before late fines kick in because the boss wants something yesterday.

The computer industry can make their products much, much more resilient than printers. After all, many people solve their printer problems by buying a new printer and that sends the wrong signal to the printer companies– a message that robot car companies won't get because most won't own an autonomous car

Much of the trouble that we encounter with our desktops are caused by the chaotic world of software. When humans download new programs, there can be any number of bad interactions. Viruses and botnets run wild because humans will click on anything. These digital infections are spurred by the incentives to hijack computers to send spam or steal money.

Car computers won't be so flexible or so open to new software. There will be few reasons for virus writers or botnets to target the machines because the cars won't have the general power of desktops. Cars already have dozens of computers big and small and they are rarely the cause of accidents because the car industry has done a good job developing them with a single-minded focus. Locking down computers in cars is a relatively simple decision because fleet managers want to ensure that upgrades only follow well-tested channels. All of these factors ensure that the robot drivers will be more trustworthy than the average desktop.

Pedestrians will quickly learn how robot drivers behave. Many people routinely step back away from the road because they don't know what human drivers will do. Each human is different and some may be distracted or drunk. People out for a walk have learned to give moving cars a wide berth and most humans assume that the driver won't see them. Pedestrians will treat robots with even more suspicion at first.

If anything, the greatest danger to pedestrians will be their trust that the autonomous cars will always treat them with deference. They'll see the autonomous cars screech to a stop so many times that they'll assume that robots will always be smart enough to stop. They'll come to see the robots as boring and predictable because the robots always obey all of the traffic rules big and small. But there will come a time when someone will be wearing black at night or some wire will be corroded or some sensor will misfire.

While I can't be certain, I remain confident that this will happen less often with robots than with the slightly tipsy driver and surreptitious texter who already make walking by the road dangerous enough.

21

Cyclists

"While traveling through the desert nearby the small town of Santa Ynez on their bicycles to camp, two teenage bicyclers are murdered by a mysterious black car. Then the car hit-and-run a hitchhiker and the crime is witnessed by the local Amos Clements. Sheriff Everett puts his men in alert and plans road blocks in the area to arrest the murderer. Sooner he becomes a victim of the car and Sheriff Wade Parent begins a hunting of the vehicle that is threatening his town and seems to be impossible to be located. When his beloved girlfriend and teacher Lauren challenges the driver in a cemetery, the car hunts her in her home and Wade realizes that he might be dealing with supernatural powers."

Plot summary of "The Car"[215]

If the pedestrians are scared of robot drivers (see 20), bicyclists have even more to be worried about. They share the road with cars during their entire ride and that won't change when the robot drivers arrive. While there are many fewer deaths overall from crashes between cars and bicyclists—623 bicyclists and 4280 pedestrians died from crashes with cars in 2010[152]—this is almost certainly because many more people walk than ride a bike.

Bicyclists, like pedestrians, will be able to draw some comfort from the robots' predictability. As the cyclists learn how the cars behave, they'll be able to trust that the cars will always do the same thing. They won't need to try to guess whether the oncoming car is driven by a grandmother, a cell phone user, a drunk drivers or someone who just resents sharing the road with a bike. The robots will drive the same way.

But cyclists may have some trouble sharing the road, especially if an elaborate system of reservations evolves that allows the self-driving cars to book their path in lanes and intersections. (See 12 and 11.) The self-driving cars can plan their routes out to the microsecond but humans won't be able to match that precision and they will probably hate being forced to watch the clock.

The reservation system could easily be written to offer bicyclists the same chance to reserve the road as cars. While this may look like a godsend for cyclists who speak earnestly about their right to share the road, the cost could be prohibitive. If the road taxes are calculated by use, this will probably be measured in seconds. (See 8.) Bikes that travel slower could require reservations that are five, ten or even twenty times longer. That means road taxes that are five, ten or even twenty times higher. The cyclists may come to rue the day that they argued to be treated equally with cars in the eyes of the law and the taxing system.

The greatest gift from the self-driving cars may be the way that all of the passengers will almost certainly get out from the sidewalk side of a parked car. Many bicyclists die when the driver opens up the door on the road side. It happens so often that the bikers refer to it with the dark slang of "door prize." The human drivers either don't look or don't see the biker who doesn't have enough time to stop before crashing into the door. The cars of the future will probably have doors on only one side to save money and increase safety for the passengers—and the bicyclists.

22

Safety

Dr. Egon Spengler Don't cross the streams.
Dr. Peter Venkman Why?
Dr. Egon Spengler It would be bad.
Dr. Peter Venkman I'm fuzzy on the whole good/bad thing. What do you mean, 'bad'?
Dr. Egon Spengler Try to imagine all life as you know it stopping instantaneously and every molecule in your body exploding at the speed of light.
Dr Ray Stantz Total protonic reversal.
Dr. Peter Venkman Right. That's bad. Okay. All right. Important safety tip. Thanks, Egon.

From "Ghostbusters"[6]

The old and the young won't be the only ones to enjoy the increased safety from self-driving cars because every age group suffers from occasional driver error. From fatigue to using a cell phone, humans make mistakes.

The computers won't get tired nor will they get critical phone calls just while merging onto a busy road. But computers might make different mistakes and the tricky question is whether computers will make more of these different kinds. Will their laser get confused by sunlight or humidity? Will their cameras miss a black car driving on black pavement at night? Google says their test cars have gone hundreds of thousands of miles without accidents, a rate that is already surpassing human drivers. We won't know definitively for some time but some estimate that self-driving cars will cut accidents by more than 90% and perhaps more than 99%.

The important differences, though, are still unexplored. All of the autonomous vehicles on the road today are designed to work with the current environment where they interact with human piloted vehicles. They're generally standalone devices that are philosophically lone wolves. The ideal fleet of autonomous vehicles, though, will be able to communicate with each other and form a hive mind to solve problems and route around danger. They'll be able to learn from the thousands of autonomous cars that traveled the same path. They'll know what's new and moving because it wasn't there when the last car came through.[176]

This ability to communicate alone will lead to a dramatic increase in safety. If there's a nasty pothole or a mattress in the road, the autonomous vehicles can pass this information to the cars that follow allowing them to swerve out of the way. This information can also be sent directly to the road maintenance robots allowing them to fix the problem quickly.

The autonomous cars will also be able to ask the cars next to them to make room for a lane change or a merge. They will be able to ride as a swarm or a herd, working together and further increasing safety. While computers will always make their own odd form of mistakes, all of this extra information will help make them dramatically safer than cars driven by distractible humans.

23

Car Lifespan

"Britain's oldest car, a two-seater Wolseley 6 built in 1904, 'runs like a dream' and has never broken down."

Stephanie Darrall, *Daily Mail*[44]

A friend of mine liked to tell the story of his father who was incredibly practical with cars. The man could fix his own cars and his goal was always to use them as long as possible until they were so far gone that they practically melted themselves into scrap, begging to be taken off the road. He routinely ran cars for 15 years back in the 1950s when many cars never got close to 100,000 miles.

One time he was too clever for his own good. He purchased a special Ford taxicab model with stronger brakes, transmission and suspension. It was only a few bucks more, but he was going to make it last for 300,000 or so miles. The first five years went well, but eventually some parts started to break. He did what he always did which was to call up the junkyards looking for another edition that was being taken apart and sold piece by piece. That strategy served him well with regular cars, but this time none of the junk yards had this model. They only had the standard edition sitting around on blocks. The cabs all expired after one or two years and they were long gone by the time his car needed parts. After a few years of buying new parts from the manufacturer at their hefty, inflated prices he gave up on the cab and bought a new standard model. The cab lasted far fewer miles than his other cars. Thrift is complicated.

Cars wear out in any number of ways. Many of the moving parts fail at a rate proportional to the amount of movement. Some of the parts like the bearings get worse when they don't run very often. Other parts like the rubber get old with time.

Fleets of autonomous cars in continuous use will change the dynamics of how cars get old. Many of the problems that affect common cars like old rubber tubes won't matter because the moving parts will give out long before the rubber dries out. It's entirely possible that a car will run through 500,000 miles in three or four years. The manufacturers will be able to use simpler parts with cheaper finishes because the cars won't be expected to last 15-20 years as they do today. The fancy two-tone paint jobs won't be necessary and cheaper paint with less expensive finishes will suffice if the car is going to only need to survive a few years in the wild. (And this detail might not matter because the cars may be repainted regularly with advertisements. See 72.)

The wear and tear will be different. Cold starts are bad for the traditional cars but fleets in constant use won't be affected by this like current cars that cool off and heat up completely several times a day. They can run hot all day and this may mean that they can go much longer before needing new piston rings.

Brakes may not wear out before the car does. If the stop-and-start city driving is ended by well-timed stoplights (see 11), then cars won't put as much stress on the brakes. Hybrid cars already use the brakes less because they recharge the batteries instead. New brake pads may cease to be necessary.

This will change the incentives for the manufacturers. Cabs are often after-thoughts for the manufacturers who just add a few changes to a model designed for the general public. When fleets become dominant, the manufacturers will want to design toward their needs and wear patterns. The features meant to entice the average driver will disappear and be replaced by designs aimed at the fleets who will have copious data identifying the parts of the cars that cost the most to maintain. The seats, for instance, will become easily replaceable because they'll be worn out first. And unlike my friend's father, the fleet owners will find their cars will wear out at a constant rate and the parts will be available at a reasonable price. (See also 6.)

24

Shape

"From artsy to zany, readers won't believe this collection of truly bizarre cars, featuring everything from the relatively tame Batmobile and Weinermobile to the Dracula dragster, phantom Corsair, and a zebra-striped Subaru. Contains more than 500 photos of the strangest, wildest wheels anywhere."

Summary of *Weird Cars* by John Gunnell[82]

Computer pilots for cars will trigger a renaissance in car design and produce an unimaginable variety of devices that get us from point A to point B. Car companies will no longer be hampered by the old requirement that the driver sits in the front, left seat (in most of the world) surrounded by glass (see 81). The driver will be in some small box connected to tiny cameras and sensors mounted in discrete locations. Everything else about the platform is fair game. Designers will probably follow the lead of stretch limousine designers who have been exploring different ways of packing people into the back of the box where no one has to drive. There will be tables for games or work, kitchens for food, and bars for drinks. Hot tubs will quickly go from silly to cliché because who wants to arrive dripping wet? But new bathroom-like fixtures for primping will be common for commuters.

Tall vehicles will grow more common as people start to do more than just sit. Some will choose services that offer the ability to walk around. Perhaps passengers will test the bounds of irony by running on a treadmill in the back of a gym car. Or rolling bars may appear complete with stools and shelves filled with various grades of liquor. There will probably be casinos, recreating that wonderful old meme of

18-wheeled casinos from television shows like "Starsky and Hutch"[74], "Dukes of Hazzard"[241] and "A-Team"[130].

Tall vehicles are expensive vehicles, though, because pushing air out of the way is one of the biggest energy costs for cars. Lying horizontal is not just a comfortable way to take a nap (see 76) but also a form that dramatically reduces the frontal cross-section of a car. Commuters may nap on the way home from work while saving energy in a long, slim car that looks like a coffin. The ride may look a bit creepy, but it will be much more comfortable than sitting jammed behind a steering wheel.

25

Safer Shells

"The Unimog generates an output of 205 kW/ 280 hp from an engine displacement of 6.4 l, developing a torque of 1100 Nm. A high final-drive ratio enables speeds of over 120 km/h to be achieved. With a gross vehicle weight of 11.99 tonnes, the Mercedes-Benz Unimog Black Edition has a payload of around 4.3 t and is fitted with tyres in size 455/70 R24....This makes it suitable for a wide range of applications: in addition to day-to-day use in the city this Unimog is ideal for excursions to rough mountain areas, remote ski slopes or hot desert regions. "

Review of Unimog U500 Black Edition from *Classic Driver*[231]

Over the years, cars have gotten heavier and heavier. One of the most striking features of the early Porsches and MGs is their extremely light weight. The engines weren't very powerful, so if designers wanted nimble performance, they had to engineer it by subtracting anything that wasn't necessary. Frames and shells were very, very light and the interiors had little extra.

Today's cars are heavyweights by comparison with hefty engines powered by plenty of gas that make up for all of that. It's tempting to deride new cars as lard buckets and hogs—— one friend with a Porsche 924 made fun of my Porsche 944 as being overweight—— but much of this extra weight adds safety even if it costs more in fuel. (See 3.) Larger frames and crumple zones add pounds. Air bags and the electrical system driving them adds more. And the engine needs to be bigger to carry the extra weight.

The marketplace has largely realized that physics are a big part of safety. One report from the Insurance Institute for Highway Safety detailed the effects of crashing together large and small cars. Even when cars are equipped with the latest safety features, the heaviest cars still won in any crash.

> The death rate in 1-3-year-old mini cars involved in multiple-vehicle crashes during 2007 was almost twice as high as the rate in very large cars. "Some mini cars are definitely more crashworthy than others," says David Zuby, Institute senior vice president for vehicle research. "So it pays to compare their safety ratings. But as a group minicars do a comparatively poor job of protecting people in crashes, simply because they're smaller and lighter. In collisions with bigger vehicles, the forces acting on the smaller one are higher, and there's less distance from the front of a small car to the occupant compartment to ride down' the impact. These and other factors increase injury likelihood."[70]

If autonomous cars end up being as safe as some predict (see 65), this endless arms race for bigger, heftier cars can end. Much of this extra weight will be vestigial because the cars will be safer. Frames can be simpler and the shell can be thinner. Most of the air bags won't be as necessary and might be eliminated.

The autonomous marketplace can also organize some mutual disarming. If the accident rate lives up to predictions, the fleet companies can come up with new standards that shed thousands of pounds. If all of the cars are going on a diet at the same time, there won't be much of an opportunity for people to defect and purchase big, hefty cars. The fleet companies with the incentive to save energy and materials won't be as swayed by the personal, subconscious need to drive the biggest, baddest machine on the street.

Energy savings could be substantial. If smart stop lights with sophisticated timing algorithms are able to reduce stopping and starting at intersections, there won't be as much energy spent on acceleration. (See 11.) Lighter weights will also help during turning. Lighter cars can also use lighter tires, saving another few pounds. They'll also have less contact with the road allowing even lower rolling-resistance and better fuel economy.

26

Insurance

"Car insurance in France must be expensive."

Review of the car chase movie "Ronin" [36]

The mandate that all drivers should carry insurance is a good example of the limited powers of government. Despite draconian laws proclaiming that everyone must be insured, one study from the Insurance Research Council reported by USA Today suggested that one in seven American drivers carried no insurance in 2009. [38] In some parts of the country, the numbers were even more staggering: 28% of Mississippi drivers and 26% of drivers in New Mexico didn't bother paying for insurance.

That could change if the public largely abandons privately owned cars in favor of autonomous vehicles owned by fleet operators bundling insurance costs into hourly rates.

Fleet operators could also exert some discipline by banning customers who abuse their machines. This is already being done by car-sharing services like Zipcar. If you don't treat the Zipcars well, you could find yourself kicked out of the program.

Autonomous fleets will socialize transportation risks differently. While it's entirely possible that smart cars will eliminate many dangers like drunken drivers and cell phone users, it's naive to imagine that computers will eliminate them all. Someone is going to need to insure against damage and the burden is going to land on the shoulders of the fleet and the company that makes the autonomous navigation software. Will they be up to the challenge?

The problem is largely political. The current system isn't very safe—Mothers Against Drunk Driving and the National Highway Traffic Safety Administration celebrated the fact that only 9,878 people died in drunk driving crashes in 2011, the first time that fewer than 10,000 were killed in a year—but the problem is diffuse.[133] There are thousands of bad actors and as Joseph Stalin said, one death is a tragedy but 10,000 is a statistic.

A fleet run by a pile of software is a centralized problem. If software authors make a mistake or if they fail to find a perfect solution—both extremely likely events—someone will die and there will be only one group to blame. This company will become a lightning rod for all of the failures and they better have a political plan for handling it. Let's imagine that the fleets kill 5,000 a year. That would be a big improvement over the current drunk driving statistics, but the emotional toll would be so much larger and concentrated that it could be debilitating. Imagine that the Google car is killing 5,000 people a year. Will the brand survive in the public's heart? Will the big pile of money survive the tort lawyers? The current system survives because it's hard to assess blame.

Setting aside some money as an insurance pool will be necessary but this raises the question of how much to set aside. We have no experience with these machines and we don't know how often they'll fail. Will it only be in icy conditions? Will it happen when some kid darts into the street at the last second? No one knows.

The worst possibility is a catastrophic failure that appears randomly. Imagine that the cars function very, very well until the temperatures reach 10 below zero fahrenheit. After several mild winters, everyone feels comfortable with the machines. Then a big cold snap hits the country and the cars fail everywhere at the same time. Insuring for this failure is impossible because they're too uncommon for prediction models.

These failures are more likely in these centralized systems where everything is running the same software. Monocultures breed catastrophes because its so much easier for the same failure points to appear at the same time. The system will need to plan ahead for handling unexpected problems that can reach throughout the system. While we don't know what that will be, we can relax a bit knowing that fleet insurance will solve the problem of uninsured drivers. Will it be good enough for the unexpected? Who knows what to expect?

27

Alternative Fuels

"Harold Bate, British farmer, thought running his car on chicken manure would be a logical way to beat the high tax on his native England's gasoline prices. And it is. ... Mr. Bate produces methane gas by simply sealing four or five gallons of chicken manure in a drum and heating it to a constant 80 degrees with a small oil lamp. The gas is collected in bottles or plastic balloons through an exit valve and stored for use. Bate also heats his farm buildings and runs a five ton truck on the gas. He claims that both car and truck run faster, cleaner and better on the methane which is sucked into the engine by the cylinders and ignited in the usual way."

Mother Earth News[27]

Let's say that someone finds a way to store energy for cars that's safer, more efficient or just simpler than the current infrastructure built around gasoline. It happens fairly often and people are always experimenting with building cars that use natural gas, electricity or even compressed air. All have some advantages but they all suffer from one big disadvantage: there aren't filling stations for the alternative fuels on corners throughout the world. If someone drives too far, they could find themselves stranded without an easy way to refuel.

The need to create a refilling network is one of the biggest roadblocks for anyone that wants to push an alternative fuel. Tesla Motors built several solar-powered charging stations for their cars to increase the range throughout California. They put six of them in the middle of the desert in strategic places to make it possible for Tesla owners in Los Angeles and San Francisco to stray a bit further from town. Six, though, are more of a vision for the future than a real plan for supporting more than a handful of cars.[61;236;240]

Alternative fuels have never caught on and a big reason is because they can't overcome the high cost of putting a gas station on every corner. Fleets of autonomous vehicles don't have this problem. Scheduling computers can track the range of various models and assign only trips that are in range. When cars run low on a particular alternative fuel, they can be sent to one of a handful of refueling stations. There's no need to build out a huge collection of refilling stations on corners everywhere if computers can schedule the trips effectively.

Fleets managers, including UPS, are already experimenting with cheaper natural gas.[158] Fleets of autonomous cars will bring this advantages to average users who won't need to navigate the complexities of finding the right filling station.

28

Corner Gas Stations

"The station was an original working service station that was built in 1937 and operated as a Gulf and also as an Esso station until the late 70's to 80's. It was a working station on South Main Street when Andy Griffith was a young boy growing up. It was told that when he was a lad, that he would walk from his house to South Main Street, which was a fairly short distance from his home, and visit the service stations there. He could have very well got a snack or a bottle of pop, who knows?"

From wallysservicestation.com

The corner gas station is easy to ignore and take for granted. You drive in, fill up and drive on. But the business has evolved in numerous ways over the years to become something that competes for its place on the corner and in our mind. In their history *The Gas Station in America*, John Jakle and Keith Sculle tracked the business as it changed from just a place to fill your car to a modern emporium filled with everything you need. They tell a story of a place that's changed from merely keeping your car running into a major source of food, taxes, and community too. [108]

Autonomous vehicles and their scheduling computers won't be impressed by signs for enormous cups of soda or discount fried chicken. They will be happy to fill up at a small, discrete pump without neon signs or any branding whatsoever. There will almost certainly be fewer of these pumps or plugs in the future if autonomous cars are able to generate much better mileage, freeing corner real estate in cities across the country.

The future fleet pump doesn't need to be on the corner or even on the main street, although those locations will still be very convenient. Perhaps the big corners will keep their role because automated cars will continue to travel down the main strips and any detour will be a waste. But it seems likely that some of the pumps will be tucked away in alleys where real estate costs next to nothing.

Moving to discrete stations without the same aesthetic demands will have some big advantages. Most current stations have buried tanks that are hidden from view and don't occupy valuable square footage. Buried tanks, though, can be an ecological nightmare. The Environmental Protection Agency even has a program to track this pollution. An annual report from 2011 counts 501,000 "releases"—their term for polluting leaks—and notes that only 413,000 of them have been officially cleaned up. Frequently, gas stations go out of business and dump clean up charges on the back of an insurance fund. Above-ground storage tanks are easier to monitor and simpler to fix.[55]

What will take the place on the corner? Will anyone need to be on the corner? Will anyone want those lots? On one hand, the corners will still suffer from traffic noise from two streets instead of one. Autonomous vehicles may reduce that noise but they won't eliminate it. On the other hand, corner rooms are usually the most desirable in offices, hotels and homes. Corner plots may still be prized for their views and not just as a place for gas stations and their large signs.

29

Convenience Stores

Lloyd Dobler I got a question. If you guys know so much about women, how come you're here at like the Gas 'n' Sip on a Saturday night completely alone drinking beers with no women anywhere?
Joe By choice, man.

From "Say Anything..."[41]

The demise of the corner gas station (see 28) won't just change real estate but it will also spark some evolution in convenience stores, one of the most durable places where we spend our money. The National Association of Convenience Stores bragged, "The U.S. convenience store count increased to a record 148,126 stores as of December 31, 2011."[143] This record may be difficult to break because each and every one of them will need to redefine its role when the autonomous car comes along.

The industry has a simple model: make it as easy as possible for people to drive in and the people will pay higher prices just for the convenience. But if people aren't doing the driving, all of that time spent analyzing driving routes and optimizing parking lots will be for naught. Autonomous cars will go where they want and they won't be swayed by cheap coffee, flashy signs, or loyalty programs. They'll go where the software tells them to go.

This will mean that the people designing the routing algorithms will do more than choose how people get from point A to point B; they'll have the opportunity to control how people get some of their calories too. They can control which stores are convenient in this new world and that could be a very powerful and lucrative position.

The evolution could follow a number of paths because convenience stores serve several roles. If people are hungry while on the road, cars could come with a built-in vending machine stocked with drinks, cookies and assorted savory items. There won't be a need to stop because the car will be a rolling store. It will even be smart enough to remember your needs and make sure to keep itself stocked. Frequent customers who reserve their car ride in advance may be able to arrange for specialty foods to be available. Routing computers will remember who likes cold smoked salmon on gluten-free bread and who wants potato chips with 19% of the standard amount of salt. Cars could even stop by gourmet restaurants and fetch a special meal before heading to pick up someone.

Riders who want food for later will need other options. Perhaps the car will offer a list of stores along the path and allow the rider to stop. Naturally, there will be advertising available to stores that want to go to the top of the list. The autonomous car could offer a catalog, collect the order and then arrange for the store to have the order ready for pick up when the car gets to the store.

30

Downtowns

"Never before had values downtown fallen so much more than values elsewhere in the city. ... these problems were the product not so much of the collapse of the national economy as the decentralization of the urban economy."

from *Downtown: Its Rise and Fall, 1880-1950* by Robert M. Fogelson [66]

When Petula Clark sang Tony Hatch's song "Downtown," the original cores of cities were wonderful places where you could forget all of your cares because economic development placed the best stores downtown. [88] Then the car came along and ruined it all by making the suburbs so much easier to negotiate. Parking was easier at the mall and so people went there. By 1997, Bob Rivers wrote a parody that went, in part:

> Just listen to the clatter of the gunshots from a Nova
> You'll be in Intensive Care before the night is over
> Those drive-bys again
> Your car is not safe down there
> 'Cuz they can strip it in minutes
> Including the spare
> While you're
> Downtown

If autonomous, self-driving vehicle will change gas stations (see 28) and convenience stores (see 29), they will also transform downtown areas of traditional cities by saving people the hassle of parking

73

their cars. When you schedule a pick up on a corner, the autonomous car will glide up and whisk you away. No parking garages, no validation, and no meters. Every car will offer a form of valet service that's better than regular valet service because there will be no waiting or tipping involved. When you schedule your pickup, the car will be there. Well, unless there's a mistake, blockage or failure.

This vision may be a bit of an exaggeration because the cost of parking will be rolled into the fee. In many cases, the cars will be rebooked to pick up a new rider, but if they can't, the cost will be rolled into the overall fare. Still, the ease of door-to-door service will change life in the dense cities. Cars will be a convenience, not an albatross.

It's also not clear that autonomous cars will bring back the carefree downtown world of Petula Clark. There are two opposing arguments about how autonomous cars will change incentives. The simplest is that low-priced transportation and door-to-door service will make dense, inner-city living more and more attractive. There will be less walking and less time spent on transportation because everything is closer. The downtowns will flourish.

The counter argument is that smart autonomous transportation will also reduce the pain and inconvenience of transportation because you'll be able to work, read, talk and maybe even bathe in the car. If there's no real time wasted in the car, why not travel one or two hours for a lunch date? This will make the outer rings and the deep country even more accessible and thus desirable. (See 38.)

Both effects will probably affect everyone in different ways. The cost of energy, though, may still be substantial enough to push more people into the dense core, helping it flourish. People who live in the core won't be spending as much energy traveling and so they'll be able to devote that energy to making the area more beautiful—at least that's the theory.

Autonomous cars and their cousins, autonomous delivery vehicles, will also make the downtowns more liveable by reducing the need for space normally used for support. Parking garages will be less necessary, if only because vehicles will be in motion for more of the day (see 32). They may even be eliminated if the algorithms for routing, scheduling and pricing are efficient enough.

Stores will radically change because they'll stock less and act more as displays. Already some of the newer urban stores are just meant to give the customer the chance to touch merchandise and try on clothes for size. The actual orders are fulfilled from some warehouse and shipped directly. In the future, the boxes will come by autonomous delivery truck.

Stephanie Clifford wrote in the *New York Times*,

> Take the "location, location, location" one. Bonobos' Flatiron store is on the fifth floor of an office building, wedged into the front of the company's office. As a customer tried on suits recently, a neighboring conference room full of salespeople erupted into cheers at some business success.
>
> However, Mr. Dunn said, "you don't need to be expensive, large, street-level."
>
> "We're not very well equipped to have 30 shoppers at once," Mr. Dunn said. "What we don't want is the corner of 42nd and Fifth."[35]

The greatest advantage of density may be economic. More people mean a bigger pool for spreading out the cost of cars. A sparsely populated town may not have enough people to support that many cars, especially late at night. Cars will need to make longer trips and it will be harder for them to pick up return trips. (See 38.) In a dense city, cars can be cheaper because there will be more of them and they'll waste less time in between trips.

31

Smaller Cities

"Nothing makes me miss the NYC subway like using TriMet."

Yelp review of the Portland public transit system. [105]

In the past few decades, major cities have boomed while smaller cities have either stagnated or begun to fail completely. There will be many explanations for the differences, but one of the common factors that all of the booming cities share is a fast, efficient public transportation system. New York City residents may complain about their subway system, but only a few major cities in the world offer one that runs all night to as many parts of the city.

The rise of autonomous fleets will change this dynamic. Smaller cities like Portland, Baltimore, and Austin will be able to offer rides at all hours at reasonable prices. They will have a flexible system that adjusts routes to destinations reducing dramatically the amount of time people waste waiting. Even cities like Chicago will benefit from the cab fleets because even Chicago doesn't have the density to justify keeping most of its subway running late at night. Only two of the eight lines run all night.

While the costs may be a bit higher where the density is lower (see 30), smaller cities and even larger towns will be able to provide a public transportation system that begins to rival New York City's. The advantages that draw people to Manhattan, Brooklyn and Queens will disappear and allow these cities to compete equally.

32

Parking

"Park Under Billboard At Your Own Risk. (Pigeon Droppings)"

From a list of 12 funny 'No Parking' signs [142]

If it's true that the average car spends only 1 hour in motion, then it spends 23 hours parked. During the day, it's parked at the office and at night it's parked at home. If there's also a third, fourth and fifth spot at the store, movie theater and gym, and the average parking spot is 10 feet by 20 feet, that's about 1000 square feet for all five of these hypothetical spots. The average family shares a few thousand square feet. If you toss in the size of the average cubicle, say about 80 square feet, it's clear that the car gets more real estate than you.

The parking space itself isn't everything. The rows that people use to navigate the cars must be included in the calculations. Ken Greenberg, the author of the *Walking Home: The Life and Lessons of a City Builder*, writes:

> Shopping malls and office parks were surrounded by ever-expanding surface parking lots. Over time, the proportion of space consumed by parking had begun to equal and then overtake the actual floor space used in the buildings themselves. The average parking space today occupies over three hundred square feet, and suburban ratios for office and retail use often require four to five parking spaces for each thousand square feet of occupied space. [80]

This is a huge amount of real estate that's often hidden from our accounting because we tend to forget that it's there. Autonomous cars will make much of it obsolete. The cars don't need to wait for you while you work or play, they can be off picking up other passengers and making themselves useful. If they're really not being used despite the best efforts of the pricing algorithms to encourage off-schedule and return trips, they don't need to park downtown or near the action. They can cluster in smaller lots off to the side of the city.

These lots can also pack the cars without wasting space on lanes for humans to negotiate. The fleets can run their own lots filled with first-in-first-out parking queues that eliminate the need for any car to enter and leave. The Skyline Parking robotic system, for instance, promises to increase density by 400% simply by letting one or two robotic lifts stash cars in slots of a big, vertical garage.[210] Another company, Robotic Parking, offers a more conservative estimate of cutting the amount of required space per car.[156] Both require robotic lifts to maneuver the cars into the slots. The autonomous fleet, though, will be able to let the cars move themselves by coordinating their movement with the parking garage control software. The cars will be able to pack themselves in like sardines and then unpack themselves when it's time to give their humans a ride.

Freeing up this much real estate will have dramatic effects. Downtowns will become denser as the parking garages are replaced by stores and apartments. The houses with garages will be able to turn them into extra bedrooms, offices, playrooms or anything but a place for a car to sit and sit. (See 38.)

The effect on the streets will be amazing. While there will always be a need for a place for cars and delivery trucks to pull over, there won't be a need for cars to sit around all day and night waiting for their human to go someplace. Many city streets have one lane for moving cars and one lane for parked cars. Several in my neighborhood have two lanes for parked cars and only one for moving cars. Much of the parked space can be given over to either moving cars or, better yet, sidewalks, restaurants, trees, or grass. It's easy to imagine that the amount of space devoted to streets will be cut between 30% to as much as 70% in some extreme cases by eliminating parking spots.

The suburban malls and office buildings will also flourish. The cost of office or retail space will drop when the suburbs drop the requirement for building 4-5 parking spots per 1000 square feet of space for humans. This extra overhead and the cost for maintaining it will be reduced although it's not likely to be eliminated. If the big parking lots are replaced by trees, grass and gardens as the malls try to emulate Versailles to attract customers, there will still be the need to care for them. Gardeners aren't free, but somehow paying for them is easier to endure than paying for blacktop and all of the global warming and storm water overflow that comes with them. (See 36.)

33

Asphalt Jungles

They took all the trees
And put them in a tree museum
Then they charged the people
A dollar and a half just to see 'em
Don't it always seem to go,
That you don't know what you've got
'Til it's gone
They paved paradise
And put up a parking lot.

Joni Mitchell[136]

The city has always been deeply connected with the meme of an asphalt jungle since the collapse of cities in the 1960s and 1970s, but that connection often misses the fact that there's often more paved surface in automobile dominated suburbs where zoning codes mandate more parking than office space. (See 32.)

Autonomous cars will change the amount of paved land in an unexpected way. Cars will be able to drive with so much more precision that they will probably wear two narrow ruts in roadways unless programmers ask them to vary their path. That could have some advantages because most of the paved surface can be replaced with short grass, gravel or maybe even something artistic like a mural. New roads for autonomous cars can just be two narrow parallel paths that stretch into the horizon like a railroad.

Decreasing the amount of asphalt or other paving will radically change the economics of road building. While roads will still need to be smooth, road builders will be able to avoid 90% of the cost of paving materials in many areas. There will still need to be full sections for passing and lane changing near highway exits, but most of the land can be unpaved.

That will change maintenance costs.

Thin paved paths can be dramatically easier to maintain. Resurfacing a road today requires grinding off the top layer and then replacing it with a hot mixture of gravel and tar. Long, thin paving tiles can be designed to be replaced easily by a crew with a truck and a crane.

Replacing most of the paving with something that grows could bring about dramatic ecological change, although that would create its own set of maintenance issues, particularly mowing and plowing of roads partially covered with grass or some other plant. Paved surfaces absorb plenty of heat, turning cities and parking lots into heat islands that continue to radiate summer heat at night. The U.S.Environmental Protection Agency estimates that urban environments are 2 to 5 degrees (F) warmer than the countryside and they can be up to 22 degrees (F) warmer on summer evenings. The agency wants to reduce this effect with cooler roofs and more landscaping, but replacing 90% of the roads with grass will help.

This combined with other ecological effects (see 36) will help urban areas become more green and hospitable. Suburbs will become greener still as the roads weaving among the little houses will be replaced with grass and other short plants.

34

Roads

Marty McFly Hey, Doc, we better back up. We don't have enough road to get up to 88.
Dr. Emmett Brown Roads? Where we're going, we don't need roads.

From "Back to the Future"[258]

For most intents and purposes, a road is a path on the ground where people can travel freely. While there are some regulations about speed and occasional fees, roads are more or less one of the most concrete symbols of our collective freedom. They are one of the few places where we can go wherever we want whenever we want. It should be no surprise that the road has come to be a symbol that means so much more than just a flat surface that can support a car. (See 46 and 39.)

This freedom, oddly enough, is one of the most limiting features of a road. The openness to everyone at all hours also makes a road somewhat undesirable—except when we want to travel on it. No one wants to live next to a major thoroughfare and that's why so many suburbs were designed with cul-de-sacs to limit traffic near homes. When everyone crowds onto the road to take advantage of this freedom, we get gridlock.

Once we start orchestrating the way that cars travel with some central authority, there will be the possibility to redefine the idea of a road. Today, we're all pretty much free to move as we want through the roads because there has been no way that anyone can keep all of the cars organized. But adding a centralized reservation system for lanes (see 12) and intersections (see 11) opens the door to regulating passage on every square inch of Earth.

Imagine, for instance, that every lawn were open to travel just like in Hollywood chase scenes. There's one bottleneck near my house where the traffic backs up each afternoon and I often sit waiting while looking at a huge lawn and thinking, "Gosh, if I could only drive over that lawn, I could cut around this stop light and get home in half of the time." The people who own that lawn wouldn't want anyone driving across it at any old time, but they might be persuaded to let a few people take a carefully designed path if they were paid for it.

This kind of flexibility already happens in the neighborhoods around the Pimlico racetrack, also near my house. Each year when they hold the Preakness Stakes horse race, attendance spikes and there's never enough parking. Many residents start charging people to park on their lawns. It's only once a year and the money is nice. The rest of the year, the lawn is just a lawn. Roads could open and close with seasonal demand. Or they might be set up for emergencies when storms or disasters occur. (See 97.)

It's probably impossible to open up every square inch to regulated travel because rocks and trees will get in the way but it will be possible to open up much more than is open now. If the path is valuable enough, landowners will have the incentive to maintain the land for safe travel. The reservation agent could also limit travel or randomize the paths to ensure that no one piece got too much traffic.

Some people may not want any traffic near their house late at night. Others will probably try to cut back on all traffic. I've attended neighborhood meetings where everyone was agitating to stop outsiders from cutting through what they thought of as "their" streets. Regulators from the city planning office would sit stone-faced in front of the crowd and try to talk them out of it, but in Baltimore they've closed some streets to traffic at certain hours. The regulation of the reservation system will end up being a job that requires a politically astute leadership.

The power to turn roads on and off at certain times will ultimately allow us even more flexibility. When cars need to travel, the roads will be roads but the rest of the time they can be parks or playing fields or anything we like. I remember playing football or hockey on the road in front of my house because it was larger and flatter than anyone's yard. When a car came, we would move to the side, and when it was gone we would start up again. The future roads can do the same.

35

Street Lamps and Safety

"Delft University of Technology (TU Delft) is currently testing an intelligent street lighting system on its campus, which uses up to 80% less electricity than the current systems and is also cheaper to maintain. The system consists of street lights with LED lighting, motion sensors and wireless communication. This enables the installation to dim the lights when there are no cars, cyclists or pedestrians in the vicinity."

From *Science Daily*[233]

Autonomous cars don't need to see a string of street lights off into the distance to plan their path. Many won't need the street lamps to see objects in the road at all. They'll have their own laser scanners, night vision and headlights to let them see. They won't need stop lights to tell them when an intersection is safe and they won't need all of those streetlamps flooding the night, cutting electricity costs and power plant pollution.

Despite these advantages, autonomous cars will bring with them their own set of limitations. Instead of needing light for human drivers, they will need central planning algorithms and radio beacons. Humans seem to adapt well to driving when the power outages shut down street lamps and stop lights, but computer-driven cars could end up coming to a dead stop if they can't get the right support from centralized scheduling software. It just won't be as robust as humans who prefer those streetlamps but could function without them.

Star lovers will rejoice because light pollution from these street lamps makes it often impossible to see all but a few very strong stars.

Even those that live out in the country never enjoy the views of the stars that were common just a few decades ago.

36

Sewers

"All the animals come out at night. Queens, fairies, dopers, junkies, sick venal. Some day a real rain will come and wash all the scum off the streets."

From "Taxi Driver" [34;197]

It seems a stretch to claim that autonomous cars will help change the nature of sewers and plumbing, but this is a surprise only to those who think that sewers carry only human waste. Many drain storm water running off paved roads into gutters where it rolls down the hill to a storm drain. The amount of runoff produced during severe storms is often dramatically more than what humans add to the sewers.

Pollution from this runoff is substantial because rainwater picks up oil, salt, gas and other ooze from roadways, even washing exhaust out of the air. All of this eventually reaches streams, rivers, bays and the ocean.

The Environmental Protection Agency is now forcing local governments to reduce this runoff. Some, like Charlotte, North Carolina, are investigating taxing parking lots and other paved areas as much as $2.10 per 1000 square feet. [217] Los Angeles is normally sunny and dry except when huge winter storms bring torrents of rain that wash away pollutants that piled up over the year. Bettina Boxall of the *Los Angeles Times* reported that the cost improving the handling of rainwater is estimated to be between $5 billion to $8 billion. [18]

Large dry ponds to hold rainwater, porous pavement and paving stones with gaps that let water drain into the ground are among the ideas being proposed to solve the runoff problem. All of these are reducing some of the impact on storm sewers.

Autonomous cars will have an even bigger impact by dramatically reducing the need for parking lots. They will also be able to use narrower roads, helping reduce not only runoff, but the heat that comes off those roads in the summer (see 33), leaving a green shadow on Earth simply by allowing the redesign of roads.

37

Detours and Repairs

"Until then I had done things my way, but from then on something stepped in and shunted me off to a different destination than the one I'd picked for myself."

Al Roberts, the narrator of "Detour" [78]

When the roads fail, a bridge collapses or an accident happens, the orange cones and flares appear. Cars detour around the problem, often slowed dramatically by the confusion and a lack of capacity on alternate routes. Autonomous cars will be able to learn about the detour before they get there and choose a different route.

This will have deeper effects in addition to saving time for travelers because road work will be easier to accomplish. There won't be a need to schedule work for odd hours because travel routing algorithms can simply plan ahead and reduce or divert traffic when the work is being done. Repairs will be made faster when there's enough of a detour to close a road entirely and not repair it one lane at a time.

38

Suburban Homes

You may find yourself living in a shotgun shack
You may find yourself in another part of the world
You may find yourself behind the wheel of a large automobile
You may find yourself in a beautiful house with a beautiful wife
You may ask yourself, well, how did I get here?

From the Talking Heads' *Once in a Lifetime*[22]

If the car made the suburbs possible, the autonomous cars may destroy them or at least change them forever into something unrecognizable. People moved from the cities to their own plot of land too far from stores or services because they knew that their car could take them wherever they needed to go. In most cases, it was faster to jump in the car in a suburban driveway than to walk down a city block to the local stores.

The most prominent features of the suburban home will change and probably disappear when fleets of autonomous cars appear. The amount of real estate devoted to the car in a typical suburban house is often more than given to its inhabitants. The big two-car garage door that dominates the front of the houses and the long driveway that eats up the lawn will become vestigial. (See 32.) The garages will be slowly turned from storeroom to workbench to office or den. They don't have many windows so the conversion won't be simple but it will become another renovation project to compete with bathrooms and kitchens.

The covered carport found in so many classic modern California homes may live on for a bit, protecting the people arriving in the rain.

Everyone will still want door to door service but the cost of maintaining the roof will probably grow too expensive when it's not shielding any cars. The driveway will still survive for people who can't be bothered to walk from the road but it may be replaced by two thin paths of paving stones to save the cost of asphalt. (See 33.) That means more lawn to mow but less driveway to fret over when it starts to crumble.

When zoning rules permit them, smart architects will try to re-imagine the space and start putting buildings closer to roads to save everyone the hassle of carrying goods. They may stop looking like suburban homes altogether and start looking like urban row houses and townhouses. The front lawn and all of its kept grandeur may be erased completely if people trade it for the private seclusion of large back lawns. Some developers will create communities built around large shared spaces like gardens or golf courses and mix urban density on the edges with rural wilderness in the middle. Everyone will own their own smaller space but the lawns and grounds will be kept in common.

Not everything will be rosy for the suburban developments. The sparse layout will drive up the costs of running the fleets of cars compared to dense regions in the center of the city. (See 30.) The fleets of autonomous cars will reduce and almost eliminate the cost of keeping a car and parking it. Suburban home owners used to benefit from the low cost of parking but this advantage will disappear. Most of the cost of getting from place to place will be in energy and depreciation, two factors measured by miles the car travels. Homes that are three, four or five times as far apart will need three, four or five times as much energy and car to offer the same services. This will drive up the price of moving around suburban neighborhoods. Suburban fleets will also offer less variety because there will be fewer people booking rides. (See 2.) If the suburbs continue to be filled with people who keep the same schedules, traveling to work at the same time, the fleets will not be able to make as much money throughout the day, further pushing up prices. (See 48.)

But perhaps all of this will be balanced when riding becomes simpler A big advantage of the suburbs may emerge as transportation becomes less onerous . Riders will be able to work, play, bathe and maybe even shower in cars. The extra time spent in them won't be as stressful (see 5) , making the longer travel more palatable and maybe even profitable for anyone able to work. For this, people may be willing to pay more to live farther away.

39

Car Culture

"A road movie is a film genre in which the main characters leave home to travel from place to place, typically altering the perspective from their everyday lives. The term can still apply to scenarios where it can be a misnomer, such as when the plot of a film involves off-road travel. The genre has its roots in spoken and written tales of epic journeys, such as the Odyssey and the Aeneid. The road film is a standard plot employed by screenwriters. "

Wikipedia[57]

In the Smithsonian National Museum of American History is a long, beautiful exhibit called "America on the Move." Between trains, motorcycles, planes and ships is a relatively tiny collection of cars. Each one of the cars is a classic, but no exhibit is large enough to hold the wonderful variety of the automobile.

For instance, toward the end of the exhibit is a section called "City and Suburb," exploring the growth around Chicago in the 1950s. It holds a Ford Country Squire Station Wagon from 1955, one of the canonical cars from suburbia, but it doesn't have the long line of SUVs that descended from it. No one has that much space, not even the Petersen Automotive Museum in Los Angeles, the greatest car city ever.

Tucked off to the side of the Smithsonian's exhibit is a screen running a loop of some of the great car scenes from movies. Actors in the clips are in car chases, of course, but they're also making out, cracking jokes, robbing banks, looking for a parking spot, eating, crashing, and many other things. The clips are just seconds long, but there are so many of them that the loop seems to go on and on.

Car culture gave the mechanically inclined a power and a role in society that they didn't have when we were hunters and gatherers. For the first decades, it wasn't enough to just buy a car because cars were imperfect beasts that didn't always do what they were told to do. Owning a car meant understanding tire pressure, carburetors, spark plugs, oil, radiator water and more. Even the most casual motorist needed to think about those things or the car wouldn't run for very long. Many of these cares aren't as pressing any more because computers embedded in modern cars solve most maintenance headaches, but these details will stop occupying the minds of those shuttled around by autonomous car fleets. (See 84.)

The romance of the open road that drove Jack Kerouac to write, the futility that carried Thelma and Louise off the cliff, the competitive drive that fueled "American Graffiti," the freedom that helped Bonnie and Clyde escape, and the failed independence that left the Porsche in the water in "Risky Business" will all be memories for anyone who trades in their keys for an account with a fleet of autonomous vehicles. Everything except the makeout scenes will be gone and getting there won't be half the fun anymore.

40

Car Design

"They use the words 'rotten,' 'bad' and 'tough' in a very fey, ironic way. Often a particularly baroque and sleek custom car will be called a 'big, bad Merc' (for Mercury) or something like that. In this case 'bad' means 'good', but it also retains some of the original meaning of 'bad.' The kids know that to adults, like their own parents, this car is going to look sinister and somehow like an assault on their style of life. Which it is. It's rebellion, which the parents don't go for—'bad,' which the kids *do* go for, 'bad' meaning 'good.'
Roth said that Detroit is beginning to understand that there are just a hell of a lot of those bad kids in the United States and that they are growing up. 'And they want a better car. They don't want an old man's car.'"

From *The Kandy-Kolored Tangerine-Flake Streamline Baby* by Tom Wolfe [253]

General Motors spends just under $5 billion a year on marketing to sell just under 10 billion cars worldwide. [126;141] That's about $500 just for advertising and publicity-generating stunts. All of that is included in the price.

That's an easy number to calculate. A more difficult number is just how much of the design budget is spent on chrome, curves, fins and other doo-dads that attract the buyer. These extras could add up to 10%, 20% or even 30% of the cost of the car. To make matters worse, the car companies are redesigning their cars more often because people are getting bored and demanding more novelty.

All of this may go by the wayside as the car manufacturers start selling directly to the cab fleets where the accountants will make purchasing decisions with their calculator, not their heart or their eyes. The famous Checker Marathon, for instance, was built between 1960 and 1982. While the company used different engines over the years, the shape and design was largely unchanged for more than two decades. The cab companies liked the consistency.

Some will find the new simplicity and stability a relief from the constantly changing arrangements of curves and folds but others will start to be bored by the sameness of the fleets. For them, there will be new novelty fleets filled with one-off designs and odd features just like the hotels that offer special suites with themes.

41

Hot Rods

"David Langham, the youngest son of a hot-rod hating father, Judge Langham, buys an old jalopy but, out of respect for his father, doesn't convert it. He changes his mind when Jack Blodgett, the local speed demon, impresses David's girl, Janie Pitts, and David makes his car the fastest in town. "

Plot summary of the 1950s movie "Hot Rod" [228]

There's little doubt that the decline of ownership will also lead to the disappearance of that customized car rebuilt with love and dedication. It will just become harder and more expensive for people to express their creativity through a two-ton mechanism designed to hurl us down the road with precision. Just as horse ownership is largely a hobby for the wealthy, car ownership will become harder and more expensive for everyone.

The market may not disappear, though. Just as some hotels specialize in custom rooms with individual designs, some cab companies will look to differentiate themselves with more original designs. Some will invariably play to nostalgia and borrow heavily from the Hot Rod designs of the 50s, 60s and 70s while others may create totally different looks.

Hot Rod lovers, and really anyone who craves novelty, can only hope the market will remain strong for interesting cars crafted by someone who wants to create something a bit different. Perhaps unique fleets will emerge and charge just a bit more for offering something besides the same old rolling container with a chair in it.

42

Racing

"It's because it's what you love, Ricky. It is who you were born to be. And here you sit, thinking. Well, Ricky Bobby is not a thinker. Ricky Bobby is a driver. He is a doer. And that's what you need to do. You don't need to think. You need to drive. You need speed. You need to go out there, and you need to rev your engine. You need to fire it up. You need to grab a hold of that line between speed and chaos, and you need to wrestle it to the ground like a demon cobra! And then, when the fear rises up in your belly, you use it. And you know that fear is powerful, because it has been there for billions of years. And it is good. And you use it. And you ride it; you ride it like a skeleton horse through the gates of hell, and then you win, Ricky. You WIN!"

From "Talledega Nights"[62]

The old adage around the NASCAR track goes something like, "Win on Sunday, Sell on Monday." And over the years, the car business has sponsored racing teams because it makes their products look good. In the beginning, the so-called "stock car" races forced drivers to race cars that are, more or less, straight from the dealer's lot.

It's anyone's guess whether car racing will continue after autonomous cars take over the freeways. While the sport of driving fast on tight turns will continue to be a challenge for humans, the audience will lose some connection to it. Today, everyone knows the feeling of driving a stock car over tight turns on country roads, but it will soon be a fading memory once the computers take over. Horse racing continues even though most of us have left the farm, but it's slowly fading from existence.

The marketing advantage will also disappear or at least change. If people are buying rides instead of whole cars, they won't be as interested in whether the Ford or the Chevy won the race. They won't have much control over what picks them up today, and an entirely different car will pick them up tomorrow. It is true that modern race cars sell any brand that will pay them and it's not unusual to see cars sporting logos for laundry detergent but it's not clear that a fleet of cabs will want to be associated with humans driving too fast in unusual conditions.

There may be some hope for racing fans. Television shows like "Battlebots" show robots armed with saws, sledge hammers and other dangerous tools fighting to the death. Perhaps humans will still tune in to see robots steer their way around the Daytona 500 track—robot drivers in cars armed with saws, sledge hammers and even more dangerous limbs.

43

Rush Hour

"You ready to create the biggest traffic jam in the history of Los Angeles?"

Charlie Croker in the trailer for "The Italian Job" (2003) [114]

The modern rush hour is one of the best examples of the economic phenomenon often called the "Tragedy of the Commons." [84] If everyone is free to use roads whenever they like, they all try to drive at the most convenient time and end up jamming roads and reducing the bandwidth dramatically. In the original example, everyone was free to graze their livestock in the village commons and so everyone did until the grass was gone and dirt remained.

The simplest solution is to start charging more for travel at the most convenient times and fleets of autonomous cars will make this easy. Some new toll roads like Route 200 in Maryland are already designed so prices shift up and down during the day and rush hour commuters pay more. Prices may rise dramatically, but roads will never fail because they're overcrowded. Autonomous cab companies can roll this variable rate into the fee. (For one downside, see 47.)

Regulation will be required to prevent cab companies from flooding streets at the most convenient times. Autonomous cars will be easy to track and it would be simple to change the tax structure to charge more during peak hours. Roads are currently funded with taxes on gas, a convenient mechanism that roughly tracks the amount of time vehicles are on the road. That can easily be replaced with higher charges for using roads during rush hour. (See 10.)

103

This taxing structure can also change the shape of cities by charging different amounts for different regions. Streets in popular downtown centers may be a bit more expensive while those in the less popular areas can be subsidized to encourage development.

All of these taxes can be fed into the pricing models used by the autonomous scheduling systems. When you ask for a price quote for a ride the next morning, the companies can present cheaper fares for less popular times and give people a wide range of choices that reward those who don't crowd the streets during the busiest times. The result may be more painful for our budgets if we want to travel at rush hour, but the trips themselves will be smoother, faster, and much less painful to endure.

44

Mass Transit

Jeff Roth That's it. My Dad's coming back in town tomorrow. I'm dead.

Deputy Halik Too bad. Tough break. If I were you, I'd get used to public transportation.

From "Moving Violations" [104]

The worlds of private cars, cabs and buses are very different today, but in the future they could easily blend into one seamless system of transportation. The advantage is that a fleet reservation system can easily group together people going to similar places. If enough people are going to one location—say a ball game or a train station—algorithms can match them together and put them all on one bus. Routes can change daily as people make reservations. If there's going to be a big conference or a big ball game, routes can be strung together to bring people to the event on time.

Special pricing can be offered to those who just want to get to an event. Instead of asking for a trip between addresses, riders can ask for a trip to an event and the algorithm will tell him or her when to be ready.

This will make mass transit more practical for many events that don't begin and end during standard rush hours. Currently, it's difficult to arrange bus lines from stadiums for the few days a year when there is a game. Reservation systems will be able to schedule buses for each event that will leave at the most convenient time.

An interesting question is whether bus stops will disappear. (See 72.) While buses and cars will be able to offer door-to-door service, it may make sense for people to walk a few hundred yards to pre-arranged stops, at least where neighborhoods are dense and many people are riding together. Minimizing the amount of starting and stopping is essential for saving both time and energy. While people may want a convenient service that picks them up at the door, for those who can walk easily, that can mean going to one spot to gather with other riders. Fewer stops will be faster and cheaper.

Fleet management will open up all of these opportunities simply by blurring the difference between a private car and a bus. When the algorithm knows who wants to go where, it can group people together to save money and time. If someone still wants a private car, they can just pay more.

45

Accidents

"'Rubbernecking' is a dramatic comedy about diverse characters stuck behind a major traffic jam. Some have road rage, some stop and smell the roses, the rest find a good time.

Plot summary of "Rubbernecking"[119]

As the number of cars grows, the trouble caused by a single accident explodes. When a lane is blocked to fix a car or rescue an accident victim, heavy traffic can produce backups that last for miles and delays that can stretch into hours. The most extreme cases may be in China, where holiday traffic coupled with an accident in the wrong place routinely produce traffic jams that stretch as far as 60 miles and last for 10 days or longer.[29;243] This is the curse of a system without a central command to work around problems.

Autonomous cars will relieve this problem in a number of ways. First, accidents caused by cell phone usage, distraction, drugs, alcohol, or sleep will be avoided. (See 22.) While it's still an open question as to how many problems computers will cause on their own, the track record of autonomous cars so far indicates that accidents will become less common.

When accidents do occur—and they will be caused by runaway deer, watermain breaks, sinkholes and worse—computers will avoid the frustrating slowdowns caused by rubbernecking. They won't be distracted by the bent metal on the road going in the opposite direction, a temptation that leads humans to slow down, bringing a backup to both directions even though the accident only blocks one.

Smart cars will also be able to reroute themselves and find new paths after learning of the backup. Once the news of a blocked road appears, cars can start moving down detours, something that humans often fail to do. (See 37.)

There will also be side-effects that make the system more resilient. When the grid is redesigned to avoid stops at intersections (see 11 13), major arteries won't be as important. There can be more alternative routes that deliver riders at much the same speeds. Today, many drivers hesitate to take detours off of major freeways because the back roads are often slower. A faster grid will provide many more options when disruptions occur.

How many accidents will be saved? The consulting group McKinsey & Co. suggested that as many as 90% of the accidents will be saved by replacing the humans with robots, a change that will save thousands of lives and, they estimate, $190 billion in doctors' bills and repair costs. [171]

46

Fun

"The MX-5 Miata, on the other hand, exists purely for the joy of driving. Sure, it has a reasonable trunk—and pricier models can be had with a folding hardtop—but at its core, the Miata is a driver's car. It's wonderfully balanced, with an engine that's willing but not overpowering, a gearbox that's one of the best in the business, and handling that makes running an errand an enjoyable experience. There are certainly faster cars, but few are as satisfying."

Larry Webster, *Car and Driver*[245]

When the musical "Oklahoma" opened on Broadway on March 31, 1943, the lyrics to the song "The Surrey With the Fringe on Top" were already a bit dated.[180]

Watch that fringe and see how it flutters
When I drive them high steppin' strutters.
Nosey pokes'll peek thru' their shutters and their eyes will
pop![180]

Now imagine that same ancient, museum-grade nostalgia wrapping itself around Brian Wilson's and Mike Love's song "Fun, Fun, Fun", a song that was written about Shirley Johnson England, a girl who really did lose her car keys after taking too many liberties with the privileges.

Well she got her daddy's car
And she's cruisin' through the hamburger stand now
Seems she forgot all about the library

109

Like she told her old man now
And with the radio blasting
Goes cruising just as fast as she can now
And she'll have fun fun fun
'Til her daddy takes the T-Bird away[251]

Almost everything that made that T-Bird fun will be missing in autonomous cars. Radios may still blast, but then again, they may even be muted by fleets afraid of lawsuits over the possibility of causing hearing loss. The cars will track where teenagers go and the old man may even need to approve every trip that a child reserves. The autonomous car will go directly to the library just as the old man dictated when the trip was keyed into the mobile phone. If the old man doesn't want to approve every trip his daughter takes, he can still put the hamburger stand on a blocked list and the library on the approved list.

The automated cars will strip away some of the freedom for young people by tracking their every move (see 15)—at the same time as they give some of that freedom back to the blind and the old (see 18 and 17). But somehow the newfound freedom given to the old doesn't seem to be in the same class of fun as the freedom surrendered by girls in cars where the radio is blasting. Getting to the early bird seating at the buffet on time doesn't seem to be measurable on the same scale as cruising past the library to the hamburger stand. The world's fun budget will go into deficit. (See 54.)

Driving a car is a skill and there's a real pleasure in learning how to do it well, much in the same way that a musician feels proud of steering a piano through a concerto. The autonomous cars will ruin all of the feelings of power, and achievement that we feel after piloting a car through some mountain roads. The cars may still give the passengers a bit of a rollercoaster ride on these hills—if the passengers request it—but it's just not the same having a machine do it for you. If anything, the feeling is dramatically worse because the ability to steer the car changes everything. When I drive the car going up mountain roads, I feel the power of choosing when to turn and when to pour more fuel into the cylinders. When I'm sitting in the passenger seat, I usually want to barf. In autonomous cars, we'll all be sitting in the passenger seat.

47

Spontaneity

Otter Now we could do it with conventional weapons, but that could take years and cost millions of lives. No, I think we have to go all out. I think that this situation absolutely requires a really futile and stupid gesture be done on somebody's part!
Bluto Let's do it!

From "Animal House"[169]

Uber is a company that matches limo drivers with people who need rides. It offers an app for fetching rides that's a precursor to the apps that will almost certainly dominate the autonomous car business. The system works smoothly but it is already illustrating what will happen when demand surges. On New Year's Eve, for instance, the prices for rides skyrocket after midnight. People who would normally pay $8 are charged $200 or more. Everyone feels gouged, but Uber remains devoted to the principles of supply and demand.[24;200]

One of the continual promises running through this book is that fleets of cars will be ready to carry people with just a quick tap on a smartphone app. That vision remains sound, but it's not clear exactly how spontaneous people will really be able to be. It's one thing for a fleet to respond to the snap your fingers when it's a gorgeous summer afternoon: it's another to deliver a great response when everyone wants a ride on a rainy, cold Friday evening.

Planning capacity to handle big peaks in demand is impossible to get right. If there are enough cars for rides on New Year's Eve, that means that plenty are sitting around for 90% of the year. If the capacity is just right for the average day, then the costs are minimized but there will be gouging at peak times. The riders need to either pay more at peak times or at average times.

The side effect of this may be to curtail spontaneity. Private ownership lets everyone get in their own car whenever the whim hits them, but the cost of this is letting most of the cars sit idle for 23+ hours each average day. Moving to a tightly regulated and scheduled fleet will crush this whim with high prices.

The best place to see this is in the airline business, the industry that's done the best at using dynamic pricing to smooth out demand. Few people fly with much spontaneity any more because the pricing model rewards those who plan ahead and buy their tickets weeks in advance. The airlines are getting very good at filling their planes and delivering travel. The prices on holidays are high but the average price is much lower than it was in the days of a flat pricing model.

This will almost certainly happen in the automated cab business. Those who commit to a particular time for commuting to work will be rewarded with the lowest prices. Those who want the flexibility to stay a few minutes longer for an important meeting will pay dearly, often with cancelled reservation fees.

The silver lining is that the old spontaneous world is not as free as we would like to believe. The roads are often jammed at the peak times and time, not money, becomes the way the system rations travel. It was never possible for everyone to just jump in their car because the roads could only support more than a few. We may pay a high cost for spontaneity in the future, but now we pay differently with gridlock and traffic jams.

48

Clusters◁

Will robot cars lead to greater clustering, self-segregation and separation? Predicting how autonomous cars will change social behavior is difficult because people are motivated by so many factors that choosing one that trumps others is often an exercise in guessing. Still, robot cars will unwrap the cost structure of automobile transportation, making the cost per mile more transparent. And that will change the way we think of where we live and who we visit.

The old model forced us to spend heavily on the car upfront, effectively hiding much of the cost of ownership. Once you own the car, you might as well use it. Gas and tolls were the only apparent cost per mile. But a fleet of robot cars (in a competitive environment!) will need to charge by the minute and by the mile. The cost of traveling will be fully apparent and people will change. Commuting longer distances will change the price of suburbia (see 38) and the more visible per-mile cost will change how people think about just driving across town for any reason (see 47).

Will this change how we structure our social lives? One of the more fascinating results from one computer simulation show how cities will become more segregated if people insist on moving into homes where at least a small fraction (about 25%) of their neighbors are the same color. [77;191;192] The fraction that created the segregated commu-

113

nity wasn't 90% or 70% or even 50%. If most of those in the simulation insisted on living near just 25% of others from the same group, those groups would segregate in just a few clicks on the clock. Small desires can have big effects, especially when people are limited to a two-dimensional surface.

Will we be more selective in where we live and with whom we share a street? Almost certainly because we'll spend more time near them. This could lead to more unintended segregation of many kinds, not just racial. People will cluster in pockets of mirror images who make them feel comfortable about themselves. We'll become more tribal and unconnected, all because of transportation costs.

Alcohol

"The difference between handguns, and cars and alcohol ... is that handguns are designed to kill people. Cars and beer are not."

Steve Read[175]

There's no doubt that self-driving cars will make it easier to drink alcohol without worrying about hurting someone else or yourself.

It's tempting to assume that this freedom will lead to more consumption, but statistics don't make this obvious. Some cities like New York or Boston have good public transit systems that already lift this worry from the shoulders of the residents. Do they take advantage of it? One survey of the "Drunkest Cities" listed Boston, but also Milwaukee, Fargo, San Francisco, and Austin.[182;183]

Town	Average Drinks Per Person Per Month	Percent Binge Drinkers	Deaths Per 100k Residents from Liver Dis.
Milwaukee, WI	12.76	21.8	3.9
Fargo, ND	12.48	21.8	3.5
San Francisco, CA	12.06	19.6	6.9
Austin, TX	13.77	20.4	3.3
Reno, NV	12.13	16.8	11.9
Burlington, VT	12.24	18	6.2
Omaha, NE	12.09	19.7	3.8
Boston, MA	14.38	20	1.3

Other statistics suggest it's not just the freedom to ride public transit. According to the Beer Institute, New Hampshire residents drink 31.6 gallons per person per year while New Yorkers consume 16.7 gallons. Even Utah with its large Mormon population consumes 12.12 gallons.[183] There aren't any subways in New Hampshire and not many buses either. But then New Yorkers drink more wine than most other states, but are in the middle of the pack when it comes to overdrinking.[68;116;214] The rural states like Wisconsin, North Dakota, Minnesota and Iowa lead the list of binging states.

The numbers suggest the freedom to drink without driving is not connected with higher consumption. While some of these cities have liberating public transit, many don't. Washington DC, the most urban state in the survey consumes almost 25% less than very rural Wisconsin. The amount we drink may depend much more on age and social choices, not the need to drive somewhere.

Still, autonomous cars will make it easier for all of these places to drink more without worrying about drunk driving—something that most may not do well enough already. The good news is that any extra health problems caused by this freedom to drink will be balanced by a reduction in drunk driving injuries and fatalities. (See 22.)

50

Eating◁

Scott Turner Don't eat the car! Not the car! Oh, what am I yelling at you for? You're a dog!

in *Turner and Hooch* [203]

Autonomous car fleets will change food delivery, transforming the service beyond carrying meals from restaurant to home or office. (See 87 and 29.) They'll also mix transportation with eating. Just as dinner cruises circle harbors and dining cars used to travel with trains, some autonomous vehicles will be set up for diners.

Some cars will feed workers on their way to the office. They'll come stocked with a minibar filled with orange juice, a coffee pot and a selection of baked goods. A robot chef will cook a variety of hot egg dishes. Cab fleets will compete not just on price but on amenities, offering the best breakfast for the price.

Others will specialize in business meals, bringing together groups and feeding them enroute to a bigger meeting or event. They'll be rolling pantries, with refrigerators filled with sandwiches, salads and drinks. Cars will pick up the team from multiple locations and let them meet and eat while traveling together.

Practically every concept from a hotel or a restaurant will be replicated inside these rolling rooms. (See 76 and 51.) There will be afternoon teas that take ladies to a concert in the park, rolling kids meals that take children to a birthday party at a horse farm, and probably even romantic dinners that circle the city or travel along any road with a view.

The food does not need to come from automatic machines or refrigerators. The cars may stop at the fanciest restaurants for a take out picnic before heading to pick up the guest. The food will be done in a professional kitchen, not some mechanism shoved in a dashboard. This will expand the options and allow restaurants to emerge without dining rooms. They'll just deliver the food to cars in much the same was as carhops did at drive-ins during the 1950s.

51

Party◁

"The Biltmore Garage wants a grand, but we ain't got a grand on hand. And they now got a lock on the door to the gym at Public School 84. There's a stock room behind McKlosky's Bar, but Mrs. McKlosky ain't a good scout. And things being how they are, the back of the police station is out!"

from "The Oldest Established" in *Guys and Dolls* [128]

If cars can be turned into rolling showers (see 38), restaurants (see 50), or gyms (see 2), why not just turn them into rolling party rooms? Limousines already serve this purpose for bachelor and bachelorette parties. There's no reason not to expect the same thing when the driver is replaced by a robot.

This may be more of a challenge than an opportunity for the industry. While cab fleets will compete to offer whatever customers can afford, there's a real risk to nurturing the worst human habits. If people drink too much, they often damage things. It's not a party, some feel, until something or someone gets hurt.

Part of the problem will be younger riders (see 16 and 15). Parents won't want to fund a system that nurtures trouble. They may insist on the power to order up instant video surveillance so they can act as virtual chaparones. And then what fun will it be?

But the bigger problem may be full adults who live their weeks stuck in cubicles or difficult jobs. They live without fear of parents and with the ability to defeat mechanisms. Cab fleets will be able to track down those who cause damage through video and other tools, but it could be a challenge if some riders don't have the means to pay for the repairs. Can they be banned for life? Or tracked down later? Will civil rights lawyers complain if some people can't travel because of their past sins?

52

Privacy and Anonymity

"The Fourth Amendment provides in relevant part that '[t]he right of the people to be secure in their persons, houses, papers, and effects, against unreasonable searches and seizures, shall not be violated.' It is beyond dispute that a vehicle is an 'effect' as that term is used in the Amendment. We hold that the Government's installation of a GPS device on a target's vehicle, and its use of that device to monitor the vehicle's movements, constitutes a 'search.'"

Majority opinion in U.S.v. Antoine Jones [188]

Running away and disappearing used to be easy. You saddled up the horse and headed out of town. Only a few outlaws like Butch Cassidy were notorious enough for the law to take up the chase—something that often failed. [163] Even when cars arrived, traveling used to be relatively anonymous and private. You went where you wanted within a country and that was your business, not anyone else's.

That's slowly changed for air travelers who are now required to register in advance in the United States. Cars have slowly caught up. License plate scanners are common at toll booths now and some researchers are even experimenting with recording the identification number given to each tire by an embedded RFID chip. Rolling down the road leaves a permanent trail. [220]

Those records can be even more complete with autonomous cars that will able to track everything we do. Fleet managers won't do it at first because they won't care much about what their customers do. They'll just want to keep track of their rolling stock and optimize the routing algorithms so everything is very efficient.

This tracking will upend the role of cars for teenagers. (See 15.) The machines for escaping parents will be turned into tracking beacons. Parents who pay the bills will be able to follow the cars and monitor where their children are going. Car companies will probably promote the surveillance as a way to give parents some peace of mind and children some security. The old feeling that cars could be used for independence and fun (see 46) out of reach of the parents will be pretty much over.

The tracking will also affect adults. Even though autonomous fleets won't care much about what you do, the data will still be there for others. In time, fleet operators will almost certainly try to use this data to sell us things. If you're making frequent trips to one part of town, they'll start to pepper you with ads and coupons for stores and coffee shops around there. If you're going to the movie theater every Friday night, they'll start sending you ads for movies on Thursday. It's going to be another frontier for data miners and marketing statistics geniuses.

The data will also be available to police and other arms of the government, in many cases without a warrant. While laws governing this new area are unwritten, the old ones can apply. The government routinely intercepts electronic messages under the FISA law, recently extended until 2017. [157;166] While these rules are meant to focus on foreign intelligence, police often routinely request business records using subpoenas or just by calling up the company. There's no reason to assume that the fleet operators will resist in any way. Many rental car companies share information with any law enforcement investigator.

It's hard to imagine that there will be any privacy left with these cars. The only option may be to ride with someone else, perhaps with permission or perhaps surreptitiously. It might be possible to get someone to let you share a ride if you plead a bit. Or perhaps people will jump on top without asking. Even this might be difficult to pull off over time because the cars will be able to sense the weight of their passengers because they'll know how much energy it costs to accelerate the car. When the cars start watching the weight of the passengers, extra riders will be impossible to hide.

53

Freedom To Travel

"The enforcement of the identification policy did not prevent him from associating anonymously in Washington, D.C. because he could have abided by the policy, or taken a different mode of transport. Although the policy did inconvenience Gilmore, this inconvenience did not rise to the level of a constitutional violation."

From opinion in Gilmore v. Gonzales

A few years after the destruction of the World Trade Center brought about tight restrictions on air travel, a computer programmer from San Francisco, John Gilmore, challenged the rules that required him to show identification before boarding a plane. The rules were not publicly circulated or generally available, but still he was asked and prevented from boarding when he refused to show some identification card. He wanted to challenge the right of the government to control how we move about the country and ultimately he failed to change anything. The challenge went on for years, but in the end the Supreme Court refused to consider his case. [189;205;206;207;208;209]

Gilmore's challenge failed, in part, because rules about airplanes are thought to be special exceptions that only apply to air travel. Gilmore could always just get in a car and drive if he wanted to go somewhere. That freedom will almost certainly be challenged when fleets of autonomous cars appear. The fleets will have the ability to kick out customers who behave badly and they'll use it to protect their property. It will only be a matter of time before others try to use this point of control to do more.

Will the right to travel around the country grow even more theoretical if almost all cars end up owned by corporations? Companies won't exclude good customers who pay the bills, but they will be sorely tempted to avoid people with a bad track record. Will they banish bank robbers who used a car to escape before? What about people who used the cars to cause minor damage? Will they exchange records with others? Will it reach a point where there's a "no ride" list kept in secret from everyone?

The government already maintains a "no fly" list that enumerates everyone who is forbidden to fly on planes. No one will publicly say how long it is or how it is changed, but people with names as common as "David Nelson" have been kept off planes. The system has evolved and the Department of Homeland Security now has a redress program where people can petition to have their names removed but the process is cloaked in secrecy. [121;260]

Will this program grow to include cars? There are some good arguments that may prevent it. First, in the process of confronting Gilmore's challenge, the courts affirmed a constitutional right to travel between states. Second, the practical reason for banning dangerous people from planes is because these people might follow the lead of the attackers who destroyed the World Trade Center on September 11th, 2001. Autonomous cars won't let the passengers drive.

Still questions like these will weigh on the minds and hearts of the lawyers running the fleets. If they gain enough of a market share, they will have the power to effectively prevent people from traveling. It is conceivable that private car ownership will gradually grow so expensive that it will become a luxury like private aviation and only the rich will have their own cars. If the business evolves this way, booking computers will end up being powerful points of control for society.

54

Sunday◁

"A neighbor, Mr Pearson, wants to take a leisurely drive with his family. Beyond his control, the Douglases join him and the drive is anything but relaxing."

Plot summary of "The Sunday Drive" from *My Three Sons*[26]

When the car was still new and roads were less traveled, one of the great pleasures of life was a Sunday drive. You packed up your car with a picnic and set out for some destination, not because you wanted to get there but because you wanted to enjoy the drive. The scenery unfolded outside your window and the world opened up. All it cost was some gas because you already owned the car.

Sunday drives in the future will get more expensive because they'll need to include the cost of the car (see 6) and the road (see 9). The decision won't be as cheap or as simple.

There will still be a market for tourism. If people want to see the magnificent canyons or mountain ranges, robot drivers will be personal tour guides (see 88).

However, to make matters worse, the marketplace for reservations on the road may evolve to favor those who make decisions weeks or months in advance. Much like airlines that have squeezed all of the spontaneity out of flying by building a reservation system that rewards locking in plans weeks or months in advance. (See 47.) This same pattern could rob us of the decision to just take a drive on a Sunday afternoon, especially if it's a particularly popular time of year. Booking a car and a lane during leaf peeping season in the fall, for instance, may require advance planning. Heading out to some popular festivals may be out of the question if you don't book earlier in the week.

The result will separate people even more from travel. Only the rich will keep their own cars and so only the rich will drive merely for pleasure.

55

Lawbreaking

Kaffee You and Dawson, you both live in the same dream world. It doesn't matter what I believe. It only matters what I can prove! So please, don't tell me what I know, or don't know; I know the LAW.
Galloway You know nothing about the law. You're a used-car salesman, Daniel. You're an ambulance chaser with a rank. You're nothing. Live with that.

From "A Few Good Men"[213]

The old joke is that a speeding ticket is not punishment—it's just a permit for going faster than the speed limit issued on the spot by a full-service government agency. (See 57.) And there's plenty of truth to this because it's easy to find a few government agencies that act like they don't really want to stamp out bad behavior completely and cut their revenues. Some U.S. states, for instance, have cut back on the anti-smoking campaigns funded by cigarette taxes and diverted the money to other uses.[71;218]

Autonomous cars will wipe out a large collection of crimes that range from speeding to bank robbery by not letting errant humans have any control. Destructive behaviors like littering or smashing mailboxes will be curtailed through surveillance. Humans in little boxes will be on a tight leash that keeps them from doing what they wanted when they could speed away into the night. Computers won't know how to go to fast, weave between lanes, or worse. We won't be able to skip paying our auto loans and then spend our time dodging the repo man. (See 56.)

But they will still be able to do some of these things—if program-mers want to add the capability—and fleets will want to add them if it will bring more money. People who need to get somewhere faster can be offered the option, but at a premium. That's because going faster than other cars will disrupt the flow. Roads, for instance, could be cleared for a fast car by slowing down cross streets. The cost of this may or may not be very high, but it's possible for the system to give some privileged status—like the old speeding ticket, reworked as a permit with a fee.

56

Debt◁

Debbi Duke, let's go do some crimes.
Duke Yeah. Let's go get sushi and not pay.

From "Repo Man"[40]

Sometimes people want or need more than they can afford. Once upon a time, the world forced people to wait and save. Then the world bit into the apple of debt and gave everyone the chance to have more than they could afford immediately, at least as long as they promised to pay it back in the future with interest.

The car industry fully embraced credit, allowing buyers to forgo saving and freeing carmakers to produce models that cost more than their customers could fit into their budget. Today few cars are sold for cash and many people drive autos that are dramatically more expensive than they could afford immediately. Instead of forcing the world to save for years, the world of easy credit lets people enjoy beautiful new cars today.

The world of easy credit only works, though, if there are consequences for not repaying. In the past, that meant repo men would steal back a car when the so-called owner wasn't looking. Today, car financing companies have evolved and are embedding tracking computers that can shut down the car if the buyer fails to make a monthly payment. Many subprime borrowers with spotty credit histories are forced by lenders to accept these hardwired taskmasters as a condition for getting a loan.

Robert Swearingen, a lawyer with Legal Services of Eastern Missouri, in St. Louis told Michael Corkery and Jessica Silver-Greenberg of the New York Times, "No middle-class person would ever be hounded for being a day late. But for poor people, there is a debt collector right there in the car with them."[39]

To add insult to injury, the boxes beep with increasing urgency when the monthly payment is almost due.

It may be a bit of a stretch to say that this only affects the poor because the repo man will come for anyone who fails to pay, but there's no doubt that the complexity of credit weighs much more heavily on people who don't have much wiggle room in their monthly budget. If anyone hits a rough spot and miss a few payments, creditors pile on with predatory fees and fines.

Debt is an impossible mistress. Most loans require fixed payments that arrive like clockwork every two weeks or every month. If you don't feed the beast, the beast eats you, repossessing your car.

The asset light lifestyle made possible through robot cabs will free the poor (and everyone else) from the tyranny of debt if prices fall enough. (See 66.) People can rent expensive rides when they are flush with cash and more mundane rides otherwise. They don't need to lock themselves into three, four, five and maybe more years of debt, just to enjoy the car. Robot cab fleets will not give them the chance to take endless expensive rides if they can't pay for them, but it will provide more freedom and flexibility to tailor their consumption to their needs and avoid the risks and shackles of ownership. Anyone can call up the limosine ride when they want to enjoy it, not just the fabulously wealthy. It will be another step toward equalizing the lives and opportunities of the rich and the poor.

57

Tickets◁

Government's view of the economy could be summed up in a few short phrases: If it moves, tax it. If it keeps moving, regulate it. And if it stops moving, subsidize it.

Ronald Reagan

The rise of robot cab fleets will destroy a significant government revenue source, tickets handed out for parking and driving violations. The punishment may an effective tool for discouraging bad behavior, but when the bad behavior disappears, towns will be left wondering how to replace the cash stream. (See 55.)

One story by Radley Balco in the Washington Post documented how some small towns ringing St. Louis collect as much as 40% of their annual budget through tickets and court fees.[9] Anyone who failed to pay or show up in court often faced extra fines, an arrest warrant and additional court fees. The story offered this quote:

"These aren't violent criminals," said Thomas Harvey. "These are people who make the same mistakes you or I do speeding, not wearing a seatbelt, forgetting to get your car inspected on time. The difference is that they don't have the money to pay the fines. Or they have kids, or jobs that don't allow them to take time off for two or three court appearances. When you can't pay the fines, you get fined for that, too. And when you can't get to court, you get an arrest warrant."[9]

Thomas Harvey is a founder of ArchCity Defenders, a group helping people fight the fines which it sees as excessive and unnecessary.

Police can also seize any cash they feel may be connected to a crime. Another article by Michael Sallah, Robert O'Harrow Jr. and Steven Rich in the Washington Post reported:

> There have been 61,998 cash seizures made on highways and elsewhere since 9/11 without search warrants or indictments through the Equitable Sharing Program, totaling more than $2.5 billion. State and local authorities kept more than $1.7 billion of that while Justice, Homeland Security and other federal agencies received $800 million. Half of the seizures were below $8,800. [185;186]

Many other cities rely heavily on parking fines. Baltimore, for instance, brings in more than $13 million each year on parking fines. This supports 95 agents who are assigned areas to patrol based upon the number of people living in the area. One watches over a region so lucrative that it's only two blocks square. [249]

All of this revenue will disappear when robot fleets start driving with their maddening attention to the rules and never parking. With the revenue will go hundred to thousands of jobs that depend, in one way or another, upon policing human drivers.

58

Murder◁

Sheldon Is it wrong to say I love our killer robot?
Rajesh As with my father I both love and fear it.

From "The Killer Robot Instability" episode of "The Big Bang Theory"[165]

No matter how wonderful an invention might be, someone will imagine how that new creation can be used – *dramatic pause* – for *murder*. Most of those ideas may come from screenwriters looking for a novel twist or ending, but that doesn't diminish the danger or the fear. Autonomous vehicles ask the passengers to surrender control and that will always make us nervous. The odds that someone might kill them deliberately may be vanishingly small, but the fear of that possibility will be amplified by our feelings of powerlessness.

There are many reasons why these fears are unfounded or irrational. Traditional cars are even easier to manipulate and sabotage. Any crucial mechanical system can be subverted and set to fail at the wrong time. If tampering with the brakes doesn't work, placing a bomb under the car is always a dramatic solution. There are few reasons for a murderer to study the APIs of an autonomous car operating system and hack the car. Some will do it, but the smarter ones will probably avoid the headache of debugging code. The dumber ones won't get anywhere.

Of course, the car doesn't need to be limited to killing its passengers. The Federal Bureau of Investigation has a team of agents in the Directorate of Intelligence who have studied the potential of the technology. They found a number of ways that the cars will end up enhancing the lives of criminals by helping them stage crimes. Humans make unreliable drivers of getaway cars, but robots don't balk at the threat of being accessories to multiple crimes. [86]

In a section of their report entitled "Multitasking," the team pointed out that criminals may be free to shoot at pursuers in a high-speed chase while the car does the driving. The "bad actors will be able to conduct tasks that require use of both hands or taking one's eyes off the road which would be impossible today."

But again, this presupposes that criminals are going to invest time in reprogramming the cars. They can't go on a high-speed chase because they don't know how to exceed the speed limit. They need new programming to break the law and anyone who will be able to do this will presumably be able to make a decent living with honest work.

Robot cars will also keep copious records about the car and its surroundings, making it easier to solve crimes and prosecute criminals. (See 89.) A good computer forensics technician will be able to dig into data and recover plenty of evidence. Enough to make traditional techniques like bombs look simpler and more effective.

59

Hackers◁

"A royal chauffeur was suspended yesterday after allegedly accepting a £1,000 bribe to show two undercover reporters around Buckingham Palace."

Victoria Ward in *Mirror*[242]

Robot drivers of autonomous cars will be perfect servants, answering to our beck and call. Humans may get tired, resentful, angry, or bitter, but robots will faithfully serve us, day in and day out. At least until someone hacks into the system and tells them to do something else.

This is, sadly, a danger that seems rather likely. Newspapers already are filled with stories about how the Pentagon's most important computers are often riffled by hackers on a spree. Why should our cars be any different?

There are some practical reasons why the average embedded computer is much more secure than the average desktop model, even a desktop in the Pentagon. Computers driving cars will almost certainly not be general machines that encourage humans to add software. They'll have one task and so they won't be as open to commands from the Internet or other sources. There may still be holes, but they'll be limited by the very nature of their design.

However, it is still worth contemplating why people might hack into these computers. The most terrifying possibility might involve murder or kidnapping, two crimes that aren't that common and aren't any easier with a robot car. (See 58.) This will always be a danger, but the nature of the crime makes it unlikely to be any more common with robot cars.

There are less dramatic crimes that may flourish, though. The Internet is rife with viruses that try to steer people to a different online store, all for a commission. This game could be played with robot cars, taking people to different restaurants or bars, for example. This seems a bit less likely to work because people usually have a firm destination in mind when they set off, but that may change if riders begin to trust robot cabs like they trust search engines.

A deeper problem may be stalking or surveillance. Robot cab companies will contain detailed records of people's movements, records that will be tempting to jealous spouses or criminals. That information, though, may not be stored in the cabs themselves, but in the cab company's central database. The job of protecting against hackers won't be any different from the responsibilities of a bank or hospital.

Another possibility is that riders themselves will hack the cabs. People have always tried to hack the subway systems to get free fares and riders will probably try this. Will they be able to take control of the car away from any cab company that owns it? One solution may be to move much of the route planning and reservation work to central servers, something that probably makes sense given that cars can get in accidents or move out of radio range. If there's no real capability to do much, robot cars will be less of a target for average hackers who don't want to do the work to take control. If someone has the ability to add all of these extra features, they probably have the means to buy their own car.

60

Regulation

"As I walk along the ramp (without a plane of my own) I look with sadness on the Cessna with bees' nests in its air vents, or the Mooney sitting on its rims with critters running in and out of it, and the Cessna 150, faded and gutted like a fish. I ask myself, how did it get to this? How could someone let their plane "die" this way?"

Barry Orlando in *Barry's Flying Blog* [154]

The age of the autonomous vehicles may come too slowly for some and too quickly for others, but it will not be instantaneous like Sept. 3, 1967, the day Sweden switched from driving on the left to driving on the right. Advanced computers used by self-driving cars have been designed from the beginning to work well with humans. Over time, though, that dynamic will change as autonomous cars become more common and begin to dominate. When there are only a few autonomous cars, computers will have to bend to humans. When autonomous cars become more prevalent, humans will need to get along with the computers.

The transition will probably go slowly. Driving on roads isn't a right but it comes close. The U.S. Constitution guarantees a right to travel but regulations have limited this. A horse and buggy, for instance, is forbidden from driving on many highways because it can't go fast enough. Similar regulations will slowly rein in those who can't keep up with autonomous vehicles.

The first regulations will probably tighten laws against drunken driving. If there are autonomous vehicles, there will be less sympathy for those who show up in court begging to be able to drive to work

137

to support a family. Courts will be able ban drivers from the roads without making them wards of the state. We may see acceptable blood alcohol levels continue to drop, lobbied by autonomous car companies embracing the cause as a way to turn people into customers.

In time, laws will tighten on everyone who deviates from the clockwork precision of the autonomous vehicle. Older drivers may be asked to take serious eye exams yearly and there will be less and less sympathy for grandpa's cataracts. Licensing agencies may design tests that mix motion with recognition and fail those who can't react quickly enough. Perhaps the deaf and those with hearing loss will also be banned from controlling a car.

The rules will eventually crack down on speeding. While many routinely interpret the speed limit with the flexibility of a yoga master, autonomous vehicles will do exactly as they're told. If the speed limit is 55 mph, they will go 55 mph. It won't take many of these obedient computers driving 55 mph in the middle lane to slow down all traffic. Who hasn't encountered a human doing the same thing, acting like a rolling roadblock? The proliferation of autonomous cars will eventually force humans to adapt to their exacting driving.

The last to go will be the rich who have lawyer money to push back against the government. In the beginning, all aviation was a private affair and many people experimented with flying, but today it is increasingly a world for the rich. Regulation has grown and slowly pushed out those who don't have the time or money to comply. The same will happen with cars. The guy with the expensive sports car will be able to maintain his ability to drive but the average person will choose the autonomous car because it's simpler and cheaper. Eventually, only a few will be able to drive.

61

Scolding

"He who controls the spice, controls the universe!"

From Frank Herbert's *Dune* [93]

The biggest danger in the rise of autonomous cab fleets will be the loss of control and freedom. While we can drive our cars anywhere we want, the autonomous cars will only drive where they are programmed to go. We won't notice this loss of power on normal trips to the mall or to school because the cars will appear to do our bidding, but eventually we will run into barriers that appear like an invisible wall.

Maybe they'll be good natured and well-meaning. "Are you sure you want to go to a bar at 11pm?" the car might ask. "You've scheduled a trip to work tomorrow at 7am. Wouldn't it be better to get a good night's sleep?"

Or maybe the car will count calories and salt, advising us, "You've already exhausted your salt and calorie allotment for the next 14.34 days. I'm not taking you out that bar that puts chips and pretzels out. Why don't I stop by the celery bar? It's just 1.34 miles north of us."

Or perhaps the car will enforce rules about travel. "I'm sorry." the car will say. "But your papers don't allow you to go into that sector."

The people who control the programming and scheduling of the cars will control much more than how long it takes us to get from here to there. The challenge for society will be defining just how much control the cars will be able to have about other parts of our life.

Traditionally, the people have often turned to their government for relief from their grievances with major corporations. But what if the government is the scold? Michael Bloomberg, the mayor of New York, already regulates one of the largest taxi fleets in the world. What is he spending his time doing? Passing laws that limit the amount of sugar, salt and tobacco we consume. What will he do with control of an autonomous car fleet?

62

Monopoly

Kitty: Can't you stuff that into a shotgun and give it to him that way?
Marshal Matt Dillon Good thing you're not a man, Kitty.
Kitty I suppose if I were I'd be just as bad as the rest of you!

From the episode of "Gunsmoke" in which an eastern businessman
tries to take control of Dodge City's freight hauling business.[42]

The cab fleets of the world are controlled by a surprisingly small number of people. Even in the largest cities like New York where laws try to push individual owner-operators, the power ends up in the hands of a few. One family started buying medallions, the licenses for operating a cab, in the 1970s and by soon after 2010, they owned 620. Medallions often fetched more than $1 million at their peak, a price that means this family was worth almost three quarters of a billion dollars just because they controlled 620 cars. Crain's New York Business called them and several other owners that together control 40% of the New York's fleet the "cabbie cartel."[211]

That price started eroding in 2014 under the disruptive pressure of companies like Uber and Lyft.[7;12] Suddenly, the government regulation wasn't effective at maintaining higher prices. One article by Josh Barro in the New York Times suggested that a seven-mile taxi ride in Chicago for $26 would only cost $11.29 in the lower-priced Uber X service.

The biggest challenge for the world will be coming up with the right rules for autonomous fleets. Competition delivers the most options for people at reasonable prices but the business world always seem to merge until only a few are left in control. If the best service is supposed to win, sometimes it wins so often that everyone else leaves the road.

One solution is to limit the size of fleets. Companies could be prevented from owning too many cars that serve a particular area. This would preserve competition but it would punish those who do the best job.

Another solution may be to create a government run utility that centralizes the reservation system, the one role that may be best served by a monopoly. This could establish a marketplace where cab fleets bid for trips. If the market makes it possible for new businesses to enter the marketplace quickly without too much onerous regulation, the city could ensure that the best cars were available to the public. The right mix of regulation, though, will be hard because there will be plenty of pressure to use the control of the cab fleet to serve other goals. (See 61.)

Finding the right regulations will be difficult. Practically every other corner of the economy has gone through a vast consolidation made possible through the power of computer networks to synchronize everyone. It's hard to argue that we'll find a way to preserve the freedom and anarchy of the open road that we all enjoy. The only consolation is that this freedom is often the refuge of criminals and those filled with malice aforethought.

63

Liability

"The truth? I thought we were talking about a court of law. Come on, you've been around long enough to know that a courtroom isn't a place to look for the truth."

From "A Civil Action" [85]

The history of the automobile is also the history of a steady socialization of risk and liability. Early drivers risked their lives and property when they took to the road and eventually a steady stream of accidents forced society to demand some form of accountability. States started requiring insurance or some sort of bond that would protect the victims of any mistakes on the road.

Spreading risks and ensuring the safety of riders and pedestrians is the biggest challenge facing the emerging autonomous industry. Self-driving cars have already driven hundreds of thousands miles without accident but no one is sure how to build a legal environment where they can thrive. On one hand, the software will never get drunk or lose vision with age. When mistakes are made, there will usually be a good video stream to settle the matter without excessive debate and litigation. (See 64.)

On the other, computers and the people who program them are far from perfect and no one knows just how autonomous cars will fail. They may make small, easily fixable mistakes or create dramatic, system-wide deadlocks that leave the country in total gridlock. No one knows what to expect and that means no one knows how to plan or budget or insure such a potential danger.

Start up companies are often good at playing the legal game. If they choose poorly, they just go out of business. If the software fails dramatically, investors lose everything and victims may or may not get some compensation. Risk taking is what startups do well and there will be a role for startups in this marketplace.

Google is no longer a startup but it brings a unique set of skills to the problem. Their technological prowess is certain, but it may be their legal team that allows their car to thrive. In the past, they have shown a willingness to push forward with technology even when laws are uncertain or forbidding. The company has ignored many of the potential liabilities of widespread copyright infringement and created a business that thrives in spite of what many see as widespread lawbreaking.

Companies that start selling automated cars will need this kind of attitude. Already, Google has lobbied California and Nevada to broaden their definition of driving to include simply giving the computer a destination. If the car makes a mistake interpreting these instructions, then someone can still sue the driver or, most likely, the driver's insurance company. In other words, it's still sort of the driver's fault.

This isn't as much of a stretch as it seems. When a driver turns the wheel on a power-steering car, the driver is trusting that the car's mechanism will follow the instructions. The computer is just a fancier, smarter version of power steering. At least that's how some philosophers would like to imagine it.

There will also be lawsuits against the programmers and the testing companies that make the cars, If the software in the cars is anything like the software in my laptop, the cars will be wonderful until they just stop working for some inexplicable reason. Restarting them will often fix the problem, but this isn't an option when you're blasting down the freeway going 95 mph.

The trickiest problem will be figuring out how to assign blame when both human and computer are less than perfect. If the tires are getting worn and lose their grip on a rainy night, the driver is supposed to be smart enough to fix the problem before it happens. But if the tire explodes because it is underinflated and the driver is going too fast, no one knows whom to blame.

The general legal environment for cars has been evolving away from blaming anyone or anything. More and more insurance plans are said to be "no fault" and the companies simply pull the money to fix things from a big pool to which everyone contributes.

Autonomous vehicle fleets will most likely take on all of the responsibility. They will effectively bundle insurance with the ride and the only question will be how much they will pay for mistakes.

The rise of the fleets will also largely fix the small but unnerving problem of uninsured drivers, a problem that defies the ability of the legal system. If people aren't going to listen to the laws about insurance, they're not going to listen to other laws. But if you don't have the money to afford the increasingly expensive insurance, you'll take your chances. As Janis Joplin sang in "Me and Bobby McGee", "Freedom is just another word for nothing left to lose."[123]

The arrival of a fleet will slowly reduce this problem by offering people the chance to book rides without saving enough money to own their own vehicle. (See also 6.) This pay-as-you-go system is common for mobile phone users who don't have the money to handle a two-year contract.

The fleet will offer a tempting, instant solution that will socialize this liability and make the roads safer.

Another solution is for the government to craft some risk pool. The U.S. government, for instance, handles risk pools for vaccines, floods, and a few more events. If the new marketplace for rides is open to all, it's easy to make the argument that the government might manage the insurance and share the risk. After a few years, we'll understand the risks well enough and the government will probably be able to step out of the loop.

64

Lawyers

> "I'm not an ambulance chaser. I'm usually there before the ambulance."
>
> Melvin Belli

Arguing about who caused a car crash is a big business and autonomous vehicles will get rid of much of the debate. While there will always be disputes over who is going to pay after a crash (see 63), the biggest change will be in the amount of debate. Autonomous cars will capture much more information and what survives will be quite useful in deciding whom to blame.

The lawyers will be the first to suffer. There's already evidence that the number of proverbial ambulance chasers is declining following the arrival of no-fault insurance and autonomous cars will hasten their departure. If there's a good video feed of the accident, it will only take a few minutes for a clerk to assign blame. There will still be a few who want to argue the facts after that. Good lawyers are necessary when there's ambiguity and uncertainty. Data removes much of that.

Entire streams of people who currently work with lawyers also won't be needed as much . Engineers and doctors who conduct forensic analysis and testify, insurance lawyers and claims administrators who try to decide just which insurance companies will pay. Most will need other work when autonomous vehicles and their firehose of data remove much of the ambiguity.

65

Emergency Rooms

"Back then, the ER was a glorified walk-in clinic, where you were seen by unsupervised interns, and residents with no training. And the community ERs were even worse. Staffed by moonlighting dermatologists and psychiatrists, or drunks who'd been banned from private practice. There was no 911, no paramedics, and if you needed an ambulance, you called a funeral home. Ollie once said: 'You stand a better chance of surviving a gunshot wound in Vietnam than a car crash in Chicago.' But he changed all that. He developed the 911 system, he trained thousands of paramedics, and started one of the finest residency programs in emergency medicine."

From "ER" [184]

According to the National Highway Traffic Safety Administration, there were about 5.4 million accidents reported to the police in 2010 with 32,885 killed, 2.2 million injured and 3.8 million crashes that "involved property damage only." [2]

If autonomous cars are able to cut down on accidents, they're going to change the parts of the medical industry built around helping people recover. Chunka Mui at Forbes magazine wrote,

One man's savings are another man's lost revenue. ... Emergency rooms could lose patients, and hospitals would lose accident-related revenue while insurers would see lower payouts. [140]

Are these 2.2 million injuries a year a substantial part of the flow of people through emergency rooms? The Centers for Disease Control counted 136.1 million visits a year, with 45.1 million the result of injury.[67] While car accidents are a small part of this larger number, they're a bigger fraction of the serious injuries. The numbers are distorted by those who use emergency rooms during off hours for what is often non-emergency care. (See 85.)

At the very least, removing these accidents will change the dynamic of emergency rooms. Chris Christoff and Ian Kolet at Bloomberg News looked at statistics from the Center for Disease Control and extrapolated that gun deaths will outstrip auto deaths by 2015. When autonomous cars appear, the two will diverge even faster.[32]

When car accident victims start disappearing, so will some other businesses. Reconstructive surgeons, rehabilitation therapists and even dentists will see less work. Ambulance drivers and emergency medicine personnel won't get as many calls. Lawyers who make their livelihood chasing ambulances will have fewer to trot after. Fewer accidents will mean fewer prescriptions for potentially addictive pain killers and those seeking pain medication will lose a convenient excuse. (See 64.)

And then there are the unintended downsides to averting so many accidents. Kevin Ohannessian at Popular Science pointed out that we're going to need a new source of organ donations. Car accidents are one of the best sources for healthy body tissue.[153]

66

Asset-Light Living

"I don't want to sell anything, buy anything, or process anything as a career. I don't want to sell anything bought or processed, or buy anything sold or processed, or process anything sold, bought, or processed, or repair anything sold, bought, or processed. You know, as a career, I don't want to do that."

Lloyd Dobler in "Say Anything..."[41]

One of the more popular business models for Internet companies is to make it easier for people to share goods. One site organizes tools so neighbors don't need to own every kind of saw. Another helps book spare rooms like hotel rooms. Zipcar is famous for helping people rent cars by the hour. Some call it "collaborative consumption," others call it an "unownership society," but in any case, living an asset-light lifestyle is easier than ever these days.

There are many advantages to letting someone else do the owning because asset-light living will also bring freedom. Owning a house or a car is a commitment. If you don't take care of what you own, you'll lose it and that loss can be substantial. The responsibility to take care of the car weighs heavily on the shoulders.

Unfortunately, it's not easy to be responsible even if you want to be. Maintenance is always a pain and it's often too expensive if you can't handle it yourself. Asking a mechanic or a contractor for a bid and then hiring them is a time-consuming process. It's better to leave the assets in the hands of the people who can develop enough expertise to maintain them.

The business will also change the flow of capital around society. In the past, people saved until they could afford something. Then the vast expansion of consumer credit made it possible for people and small businesses to own the goods before they earned enough to afford it. They would borrow and pay off the car loan.

The rise of an asset-light lifestyle will mean that consumers have less need for credit. The people who use Zipcar today don't need auto loans—although they can run up a credit card bill by renting the car. This saves the consumer from making long, multi-year commitments to cars (and other goods). We won't need to guess how often we'll drive over the next 10 years before buying a car and making a ten-year commitment to it. Asset-light living means our only commitment is as long as the reservation. (See 56.)

While this sounds wonderful, it also promises to hide the real costs from the user. The best businesses earn their profits by providing something desirable and then charging more for it. The best autonomous car companies will charge us more to make a profit. This won't be a bad thing, though, if they're able to save us more by taking the weight of maintenance (see 8) and borrowing costs (see 6) off our shoulders.

67

Throw Away Cars

It's just a car I bought myself, and kept running myself. No help from anyone else. I started looking in February '09, and only found a good one in April. The exact one I wanted, with all the options. I withdrew my life savings in $100 bills and ran home from the bank, afraid of getting robbed for the small brown envelope I stuffed in my front pocket. My hand shook when I signed my name on the title. After taxes, registration fees and an oil change I had less than $100 dollars left. I drank Olde English —or nothing at all for the rest of the summer. I didn't care.

Derek Kreindler in *The Truth About Cars* [122]

How many times have you said "Hey, it's a rental"? Okay, maybe someone as responsible and full of devotion to the commonweal as you would never say such a thing, but certainly you met such a character at a party or when you were in college.

Maybe, you're the responsible type who religiously changes the oil in your car and keeps its neatly vacuumed and detailed—- habits developed while saving for your first car in high school or college by working odd jobs.

The rise of the autonomous fleets will decimate that tradition, one of the first steps toward adulthood and responsibility for many.

Cars have grown to be either the first- or second-largest asset that many people own. Their investment can span decades and the attachment is often stronger than many other possessions.

All of that responsibility and devotion won't be necessary when good rides are available on demand. There won't be any reason to save thousands of dollars just to earn the freedom to travel where you want and when you want to. Anyone with a mobile phone and few dollars on account will be able to get where they want to go.

68

Optional Travel

> "Is there a logic, a rule to all this coming and going, all this disloca-
> tion? Is there a way to stay put, to embrace the present with every
> cell? I don't know. There are clues; as with any disease there are
> patterns, possibilities. Exhaustion, loud noises, stress, standing up
> suddenly, flashing light—any of these can trigger an episode. But:
> I can be reading the Sunday Times, coffee in hand and Clare doz-
> ing beside me on our bed and suddenly I'm in 1976 watching my
> thirteen-year-old self mow my grandparents' lawn."
>
> Henry from Audrey Niffenegger's *The Time Traveller's Wife* [146]

When a friend of mine sold his car and started riding his bike to
work, he began using Zipcars for all extra travel outside of the range of
his bike. That changed his attitude toward going anywhere. Suddenly,
he wasn't just driving to dinner and consuming a bit of gas from a
tankful he bought a week ago, he was booking a car at $9 an hour. Was
the trip worth $9, $18,$27 or, perish the thought, $36? If the restaurant
was crowded and pokey, was he going to be late returning the car and
suffer a terrible fine? Was the movie a quick 95-minute express or a
three-hour long indulgence for a director who fell in love with every
shot? Sure, the epigram that "Time Is Money" was true before he
switched to Zipcars, but it became obvious after.

Fleets of autonomous cars run by sophisticated reservation systems
may change our casual travel. Riders won't be counting the hours like
Zipcar users, but they'll still be counting the trips. Not only will spontaneity become more difficult, especially at times of high demand like
Friday afternoons in the summer (see 47) but optional trips will start to

155

sport a price tag. How we think about where we go will become more economic and mercenary.

This type of thinking has always been more common in the biggest cities where people live without cars and rely upon cabs, buses and trains. Going some place always had a price tag. Now, it will come to the suburban world and this will change all of the real estate built upon the idea that people will just drive over and park. (See 48.)

Stores and malls will be among the most affected. They were designed from the beginning to make it easy for someone to drop by casually and stay as long as they wanted. Stores wanted to be in the mall because the other stores would attract customers and they would all prosper. Now, if the cost of travel is spelled out and the shoppers make reservations for a return trip, there won't be as much value in the casual customer. People will dart in, make their purchase and dart out.

Or people may not show up at all. If a Zipcar costs $9 for an hour, suddenly paying $4.95 for shipping isn't a bad deal. Even paying $8.95 is cheaper than actually renting a Zipcar for $9. It's nice to get out and browse through a mall, but why bother if it's going to cost more.

Malls and shopping districts may start offering free travel and hide the costs in the merchandise in much the same way that online stores offer free shipping. This might be a bit harder for the physical stores to calculate because they won't know if people are actually spending any money because the riders might just be looking for an excuse to get out of their house. One way around this may be to offer free trip coupons that people can use on their next trip. Or perhaps just free trips home for good customers. Casinos, after all, track their bettors and often send coupons for free rooms to those who should be profitable. So, the free offers will just hide the real costs. If you buy something, the store will pick up your ride home and if you don't, you'll pay for it yourself. Of course, you'll pay either way, but it always feels nice to pretend that you're getting something for free. That's the kind of incentive that people need to make the decision to buy.

69

Paths

At the beginning of the movie "L.A. Story", Steve Martin heads off for work cutting through back alleys, parking lots and a dozen other shortcuts in a joking homage to the way that people in Los Angeles find sneaky paths around the long lights and tied-up streets.

The route-finding software in autonomous cars is going to change the way cars flow through the city. The software doesn't always recognize the major arteries and it might not think twice about sending some large 18-wheeler down a small alley, just because the data crunching shows that it's shorter. Sleepy neighborhood streets were once ignored by everyone except the true locals who knew of the short cuts, but computers know everything. They know that the tiny alley is more than just a way for people to get to their garages—it's a quick path around three long stop lights, two stop signs and a long path around a factory. Even after the stoplights disappear (see 11), the computers will still know the shortest path and these may be back alleys and shortcuts.

There will be many advantages to people passing through these once unknown, sleepy shortcuts. The city roads will be able to support a much greater flow of traffic. More viable paths mean more ways for cars to get where they're going without waiting for some other car in front of them. The paths will be more direct with less backtracking and fewer distortions. Shorter trips are also faster trips and more fuel efficient trips.

The people living in the neighborhoods will almost certainly revolt. Much of suburban planning is designed to let people live on small streets with minimal traffic. Even many urban streets are meant to be thinner, slower and only for local traffic. No one wants the 18-wheelers coming down the street unless they're going to deliver something.

The routing algorithms can easily be modified to place a penalty for using some streets, but activating this will require a political decision by municipalities to encourage or discourage traffic on some roads. Who gets to discourage traffic and who doesn't? The negotiations may be simple and it will depend upon the general speed of the road network. Closing roads to through-traffic will slow the roads. If everyone is happy enough with the speed, the decision will be successful.

There will probably be some neighborhoods that have small streets but happen to sit near a bottleneck where traffic would like to flow. These won't be as common in the outer suburbs where the road network was designed with central arteries, but they will probably be found in older cities. Places like Little Italy or Chinatown in Manhattan are also near major transportation paths like the Manhattan Bridge. Limiting flow through these neighborhoods could slow the grid down much more than others and the political decisions will be harder to make.

There will be technical compromises. The car companies can continue to make quieter cars that won't be as disturbing. The residential neighborhoods might only be restricted during certain hours, perhaps during the night. The cars could use a different speed limit at certain times. In the future, each neighborhood could set a variable speed limit and noise limit that varies according to the needs of the residents. Agreeing upon this may be difficult but it will offer a compromise that opens up large parts of the road network to travel. The new paths may seem as silly as the ones that Steve Martin takes in the beginning of "L.A. Story", but they've got to be worth it. The computer algorithms say so.

70

Mapping◁

Dr. Emmett Brown Things have certainly changed around *here*.
I remember when this was all farmland as far the eye could see.
Old man Peabody owned all of this. He had this crazy idea about
breeding pine trees.

From "Back to the Future"[258]

New York City's Broadway may date back as far as 1642[47;97;239]
and it may seem quite permanent to many because it's been carrying
people and goods from the tip of Manhattan to Westchester county
for more than 450 years. But to the autonomous car, it's a constantly
changing arrangement of pavement and obstacles. There are new signs,
new surfaces, new potholes and new barriers all of the time. How will
the autonomous fleet keep track?

It will update itself. Robot cars will talk to each other and track
the constantly evolving tapestry of city roads. They'll know when potholes appear; they'll ask for them to be fixed; and then they'll know
when they really are fixed. When new buildings appear, cars driving
by will be the first to notice new construction and the first to detect
when construction is finished.

Some of this information will need human reinterpretation, but
most will be fed right into a big, aggregated model of the world. This
is just one way that cars will communicate with each other and remake
the world.

This sensing will also be useful to others. Indeed the fleet may
make a substantial amount of money reselling the data it gathers. (See

93.)

71

Shopping

Mel At least he knows what he's doing. And he's in a good college.
I'd like to see you have a little bit of direction.
Cher I have direction.
Josh Yeah, towards the mall.

From "Clueless"[90]

Autonomous cars will change the roles of convenience stores (see 29) and the corner gas station (see 28) from the beginning. The general nature of shopping will soon follow, although not as quickly.

Some people will hand over all control from the beginning. Autonomous cars will be like search engines for the real world. If someone wants to try on a new pair of pants, they can type this into their smartphone and the autonomous car will take them directly to the store. The car will turn into a browser for real world things instead of web sites. Is it any wonder that Google is a pioneer in this world? (See 73.)

Others won't surrender as easily. Shopping is often a sport for some, an excuse to get out into the real world and browse items, see people, enjoy a lunch, and simply wander. It's not just about acquiring some object, but an excuse to explore and learn. Not everyone falls into this camp, but for those that do, the autonomous car won't remake shopping. It will just be a way to get to a shopping nexus. (See 30.)

Shopping centers won't disappear but they'll need to be even more entertaining and inviting to drag people out of their cocoons. Stores will become more outrageous, overdesigned and immersive. Manufacturers will follow the example of Apple more closely by building elaborate sets for their products and then limiting pricing online to prevent people from undercutting the retail theater.

Stores that do this successfully will avoid giving away power to autonomous routing algorithms. They'll survive and they may even form partnerships with autonomous fleets. People who stay at home don't use cars at night. Smart shopping centers will create enough distractions to lure them. Savvy real estate companies may even be able to get a cut from fees that their destinations generate and car fleets will pay them or watch their cars gather dust at night.

72

Advertising

"Advertising is based on one thing: happiness. And do you know what happiness is? Happiness is the smell of a new car. It's freedom from fear. It's a billboard on the side of a road that screams with reassurance that whatever you're doing is OK. You are OK."

Don Draper from "Mad Men"[247]

Every few years, a company announces that it will pay people to plaster their cars with ads.[147] In return for wrapping your car with their ad, a company might pay you several hundred dollars a month. It's supposed to be like free money, although I've never seen many cars with the wraps.

That will be different in the future. If car owners don't want to drive billboards, car fleets and their accountants won't be so self-conscious. Autonomous fleets are going to use the real estate on the cars to generate even more revenue and they'll have many advantages over current models. They'll know everywhere their cars go and they'll be able to report this data to the advertiser. Today, the advertiser just has to cross some fingers and hope that the car won't be parked in some garage.

It won't be guaranteed. If the autonomous cars lose their windows (see 81), there won't be many people on the freeway who will see them. Even if the windows stay, the riders inside have no reason to look out the windows because they'll be playing games or getting work done (see 82). The driver used to scan the roads looking at everything, but only the computer will be doing that. Perhaps the only value will be for ads on cars circulating in the dense downtowns with plenty of people on the sidewalks. The car's computers could probably count these people too and provide an estimate of how many eyeballs saw the ad on the car with a scary amount of precision.

The same effect will haunt real estate. The value of billboards will almost certainly crash. Bus stop ads could disappear but then again they might not if bus stops survive. (See 44.) Some buildings next to freeways are effectively billboards for their companies and their value will drop if the riders don't bother to look up. In general, the riders will probably be more distracted by the card games and work inside the car to pay much attention to what's passing by, at least on common routes.

The real action will be inside the cars. The advertisers will need to look for other ways to influence the riders and that will mean getting inside the car. (See 73.) The advertisers will probably need to cut deals with the autonomous car companies that will end up acting like search engines for the real world. (See 71.) This may be why Google is so drawn to creating their own cars.

73

Marketing◁

> "Among car companies, which are displaying their latest products at the Paris Motor Show now under way, there is a growing recognition that young people may simply not care about cars as much as their elders. Smartphones now rival automobiles as the default symbol of adulthood, and the portals to the world beyond home and school."
>
> Jack Ewing in the *New York Times* [58]

On one hand, autonomous cars will upend and perhaps destroy the world of display advertising by letting passengers read, sleep, talk or do anything but look out the windows at billboards, neon art, or guys dancing on the street corner trying to get you to read their sign. (See 72.) On the other, it will create new marketing mechanisms . Cars will be portals to the physical world and control of the portal will be sold to the highest bidder. While riders will still be nominally in control of where cars go, autonomous cars will be able to subtly and not-so-subtly influence that decision. At the very least, the booking software will be search engines that take people to stores or sources, not just addresses. People won't just ask for "1313 Mockingbird Lane," but "pizza" or "beer" or even "sports bar with a license to display the current football match from Argentina." They'll be search engines for meet-space. (See 71.)

There will be many opportunities for collaboration between attractive destinations and cabs. Fleet owners may sponsor free concerts in the parks during off-hours when their cabs are dormant, knowing they'll make enough on selling rides to the concert. Or perhaps the destinations will pay for free rides to attract people just as casinos often pay for free rides. Ryanair, the Irish-based low-cost carrier, is known for embracing a business model where the destinations subsidize the cost of the flights. Cities on both ends will make more through tourist revenue and taxes, a carrot that Ryanair uses to argue for lower taxes on plane tickets. With the right subsidies, Ryanair may lower transatlantic flights to 10€.[20;33;201]

This will be just the beginning because passengers will be a captive audience. Autonomous car fleets could start off putting ads inside the cars. Cabs today often have ads plastered on the bulletproof divider and autonomous cabs will probably try something similar. Basic displays, no matter how clever, will probably have a limited success. They'll clutter the aesthetics of the cab interior and hurt the fleet's ability to market a comfortable and relaxing ride. Unless the pay is high, the ads will probably disappear.

Some fleets may borrow from airlines and railroads which run their own magazines. A print or digital version that's just waiting for a bored passenger should command good rates. A digital version could tune the content to the route and the destination.

But even more sophisticate opportunities are available. Cab fleets may offer free rides to anyone willing to take surveys or interact with some advertising. There will be plenty of captive time and not all riders will have their own work.

The best opportunity may be taking advantage of the physical space. The marketing in the cabs doesn't need to be simple, old and flat rectangles. Cabs are physical spaces and they can hold physical things. They can offer display models of new products or samples of tactile items like fabric. They can be filled with interactive kiosks that engage the rider in ways that search engine ads can't do. The cab can be a portal to the physical world in so many ways.

74

Radio

"Oh, pardon me. For some reason you sounded a little taller on radio."

Buford T. Justice from "Smokey and the Bandit" [145]

The AM/FM radio and the car go together. Cassette tapes, 8-tracks and iPods can deliver music, but radio stations provide news, traffic, weather, music and occasionally a live human voice to break the tedium.

According to a survey by Edison Media Research and Arbitron in 2003, 33% of all radio listening in the United States was done in the car. [230] That was in 2003, just after the iPod was introduced and that number has only grown as Internet services like Pandora take over the home.

Autonomous cars will probably push FM and AM radio's ad-driven format over the cliff along with billboard advertising (see 72). Listening is all the human driver can safely do, but passengers are free to read, watch video, play with their mobile phones or work.

There will be a demand for music, but autonomous fleets will be a gatekeeper. In the past, musicians have insisted on royalty payments from businesses like restaurants that play the radio. Autonomous car fleets may find they have enough power to push back and charge music companies to play songs and promote artists. Or, maybe the fleets will give up and leave the job of entertainment to mobile phones and tablets.

Self-driving cars will also be aware of and able to avoid traffic problems (see 43), eliminating the need for live traffic reports, one of the main reasons left for tuning in. Radio stations make most of their ad revenue during rush hour when they lure people in with traffic and news, the reason why Arbitron calls AM/FM radio the "soundtrack" of billboard advertising and the combination "one of the last messages a consumer receives before making a buy decision."[5]

Companies that sell to people buying dinner on their way home need that voice and they need to advertise before people make a decision. Cars may give up entertainment but they'll have even more control the way that people decide what they buy for dinner or where they shop. (See 29 and 28.) Ride-scheduling software will take over the role radio found it had. This advertising power may be so valuable that the rides may be heavily subsidized or even given away in return for routing people to the right stores or restaurants. That power could be more lucrative than radio ever was but that software probably will never have the same charm or quirky humanity as late night DJs idolized in movies like "American Graffiti" or in television shows like "WKRP in Cincinnati" or "News Radio."

75

Signs

"I think that I shall never see a billboard lovely as a tree. Perhaps, unless the billboards fall, I'll never see a tree at all."

Ogden Nash [144] after Joyce Kilmer [91]

The path from here to there is almost always lined with signs. Roads winding through the wilderness or the prairie may not have many of them, but everywhere else is filled with big, wordy placards filled with instructions and seductions. As Les Emmerson wrote in his song, "Sign, sign everywhere a sign/ Blocking out the scenery breaking my mind/ Do this, don't do that, can't you read the sign?" [54]

Many of these signs and certainly the biggest of them are there for the eyes of the driver. Road signs with street names help the driver find the right path. Businesses have signs that help drivers choose them. Huge, glaring lighted signs on long poles beckon drivers with an empty stomach or a full bladder to pull off the road.

All of these won't be necessary when humans aren't guiding the cars. They'll choose the destination before getting in the car and the car will find its way without big, flat boards covered with human-readable words and pictures. GPS satellites and inertial guidance systems will do the job. Passengers will be able to look out the window and be drawn to a sign, but the odds get longer when there's no driver forced to keep looking. Everyone may be reading a book, watching a video or sleeping. (See 76 and 81.)

Views of nature will get prettier and the sights will probably get more harmonious as businesses have less reason to battle for our attention with larger, brighter or more visually irresistible displays. Some of this will be a big improvement, but there will be a sad nostalgia for the best of the signs. We may not miss the dumb or the tasteless, but there will be nothing that will replace huge roadside attractions like five-story bowling pins, lumberjacks, cowboys, cattle or long extinct dinosaurs.[4;19;109;120]

76

Overnight Travel

> "I've heard that if you take off one sock and one shoe, it's harder for your body to regulate your temperature and therefore harder for you to get comfortable enough to fall asleep. Don't know if it's true, but it's certainly worth a try!"
>
> Internet advice on how to drive all night to Disney World. [167]

A friend once described an overnight trip from college in Nebraska to New York on the Wednesday before Thanksgiving. It went something like this, "It took about 20 hours because we had to go to a last class on Tuesday afternoon. The professor was such a jerk. We took turns driving and didn't stop until we got home. It was pretty cool, but we had to drink lots of coffee and open the windows about eight times at night to stay awake. But we made it."

Contrast that with a trip that I once took from Edinburgh to London. I got on the train at 11pm and slept in a bunk until I woke up in London the next morning. The trip took around 6 hours and we arrived around 5am, but they didn't force us to get up immediately. We could take our time while the train was parked in the station.

Autonomous cars will turn the first kind of trip into the second. Car travel at night does not need to be uncomfortable. Fleet owners can learn from sleeper cars on trains and provide services that deliver people rested on the next day. The sleeper cars may be a bit more expensive but the smart fleet company will price them at less than the cost of a hotel room.

Car rides of 8-10 hours make it possible to go to sleep in Washington, D.C., and wake up in Chicago or go to sleep in Los Angeles and wake up in San Francisco. It won't be free because of the costs of energy, but there won't be a need to waste the time in transit.

One challenge will be creating a safe and comfortable bunk. Railroad sleeping cars went through many iterations. George Pullman, the man who made his fortune perfecting the sleeping car, started tinkering with them in 1858 and continued improving them for the rest of the century. [37;99] Early models were often too short, too wide or too expensive, but in time the company standardized on a design with bunks that would pull-down much like luggage racks.

It's worth noting George Pullman never owned a railroad. Joe Welsh, Bill Howes and Kevin Holland wrote in their history:

> Though a major player in American passenger railroading for more than a century, Pullman was not a railroad. The company built, owned and leased a large fleet of sleeping and parlor cars, which it provided to the railroads under contract. The railroads handled the reservations and carried travellers from place to place aboard Pullman cars. Pullman was essentially a giant hotel company. [248]

The same split in corporations may evolve in the world of autonomous cars. Perhaps hotel companies will extend their brands by creating rolling Hilton rooms or a rolling Ritz. These pods can be placed on sleds driven by autonomous cars owned by transportation companies. (See also 77.) Passengers will be able to choose different rooms for night travel just as they do when they pick between hotels.

One of the early debates was whether to sleep with the head or the feet toward the front of the train. The early Pullman manuals suggested that riding with the head first was better because any cinders drifting through the windows would land by the feet instead of the face. When air conditioning arrived, many switched to riding with their feet in front in case the train stopped suddenly. [202]

A safer overnight autonomous car might arrange the bunks with the feet in front and a flexible netting that stretches over the blankets to keep the rider in the bed if the car flipped over or turned suddenly. Well-padded sides would also help. This may not be perfect, but it would almost certainly be safer than driving all night amped on coffee with cold air gusting through the windows.

77

Pods

"General Motors sees a future where people navigate crowded cities in big Segways that look kinda like a Dyson vacuum cleaner and can drive you home when you've had one too many."

Stuart Schwartzapfel in *Wired* [198]

Cars and taxicabs today are one unit purchased with coach and engine married together in a way that no man will ever tear asunder largely because it's almost impossible to do any maintenance on a modern car's engine compartment. It takes a skilled mechanic several hours just to replace the spark plugs today let alone remove an engine.

There's no reason why this needs to remain true in the world of autonomous vehicles. Railroads have always separated the engines from the cars where people and freight ride. Pods for people will be dragged around by smart engines. [160]

Separating the two roles has many advantages. Stronger engines can be built to take cars up mountains while smaller ones can move the same pods around cities. Fixing the seats won't mean leaving the engine doing nothing and vice versa. If the big economic value of autonomous cars is severing the bonds between the car and the owner, another gain will be splitting the riding compartment from the engine.

Pods can be shuffled around like train cars. They may move quickly around the city with minimal engines when they're going in different directions. When they travel in packs on the highway, they can be linked together in a long line and pulled by a bigger, even more efficient engine. These long chains of pods will draft each other to overcome wind resistance. Baggage or freight going to the same destination can be attached to the same train, further pooling the cost of energy. This same combination of freight and passenger travel could work well in short trips around the city, too, because autonomous engines could be programmed to handle much of the last-mile delivery work of the postal service. (See 87.)

Separating the travel compartment will also allow engines and pods to evolve separately to satisfy different markets. Pods will almost certainly come in different grades of luxury and sport designer brands.[227]

Some may choose to own the pod travel in each day. While this can be more expensive than just riding in a pod run by others, humans like to control their own space. They will be able to choose their own upholstery and in time it will adapt to their bodies, much like a favorite chair. Riders that can afford to let their pod sit unused for the day and who have a parking spot for it may choose the luxury of controlling their own pod. Some people may not want to share. They can keep all of their stuff in the pod where it is always where they expect it to be. (See 79.)

While these pods will grow in complexity and luxury, the romance of the engines, though, will fade. In time, few will understand what Jim Jacobs and Warren Casey were thinking when they wrote the lyrics to "Greased Lightning" for the musical *Grease*:

> We'll get some overhead lifters and some four barrel
> quads, oh yeah
> Fuel injection cutoffs and chrome plated rods, oh yeah
> With a four-speed on the floor, they'll be waiting at the
> door[107]

In the future, only the fleet engineers and their CFOs will care much about the engine's power and efficiency and even then they probably won't be moved to sing or dance about the new engine that's 4.3% more efficient than last year's model.

78

Extra Power◁

Neil McCauley A guy told me one time, "Don't let yourself get attached to anything you are not willing to walk out on in 30 seconds flat if you feel the heat around the corner."

From"Heat" [134]

In the garage of every suburban home is a heating plant that gives off free electricity when it runs. It's also the reverse. An electrical generator that gives off free heat. Homes, however, don't use any of this capacity, though, because most are wired to use electricity from a distant generating plant and heat from burning something entirely different. Why are there two systems?

While most of this book assumes that robot cars will operate continuously as a fleet of cabs, there's a possibility that some will find off-peak work heating and powering homes. That will help eliminate the need to push electricity long distances from far-away powerplants and save the power lost to transmission line resistance because the generators will be parked throughout the neighborhood.

Nissan, for instance, is already talking about using the battery of their electric car, the Leaf, to power homes. The car would absorb electricity when power is cheap and deliver it during times of peak demand. [235;257] This simple model, though, could be easily extended to capture both heat and power from conventional engines.

This scheme offers a simple advantage: cars will naturally follow people to work or school and then home at night. They'll naturally be close to the people who need power and heat. When there are more people in a neighborhood, there will also be more cars feeding power into the grid and heat into the homes.

Current infrastructure already offers some support. Many homes have large tanks filled with number 2 fuel oil which is close to the same formulation as diesel fuel. Others have natural gas pipes that can supply cars if their engines are modified to use natural gas.

Those cars will be able to deliver both transportation for people, delivery services for goods, heat for homes, and electricity for neighborhoods. They'll go where they're needed and then, like the character in "Heat", move on with 30 seconds notice.

79

Trunks◁

"Paul and Sarah are two low level technicians on the deep space exploration ship The Eurydice. The ship explodes and the two find
themselves the only two survivors on an escape pod built for one.
There is no hope of rescue but an unlimited supply of air, water, and
food. Hell is other People."

Plot summary of *The Pod*[112]

A friend of mine is an architectural photographer. He doesn't have
much of an office, though, because he's on the road so often taking
pictures of buildings. His equipment is usually stored in the trunk of
his car, hidden from view but easily accessible. He is a good example
of someone who won't benefit from the emergence robot cab fleets
because he won't want to load his equipment at the beginning of the
day on the way to an assignment and then reload it again at the end of
the day when it's time to go home.

However, here will be solutions. Just as some private seating pods
will emerge that can be shuffled and towed by cars or engines (see
77), there will also be trailers that carry people's things. They will be
attached at the beginning of the ride and detached at the destination.
If they're designed well, they may even be picked up and dropped off
without any human intervention.

While these trailers or moveable trunks will largely be designed
for people to store their tools, clothing, equipment and other kit, they
could also serve a role in the delivery of goods. A big delivery could be
dropped off in a trailer or a trunk in front of someone's house. When
they're finished unloading the goods, they could notify the company

which would dispatch another engine to pick up the trailer. (See 87.)

80

Manufacturing

"Car, windshield. Drudgery piled atop drudgery. Cigarette to cigarette. Decades rolling through the rafters, bones turning to dust, stubborn clocks gagging down flesh, another windshield, another cigarette, wars blinking on and off, thunderstorms muttering the alphabet, crows on power lines asleep or dead, that mechanical octopus squirming against nothing, nothing, NOTHINGNESS. I wanted to shout at my father, 'Do something else!' Do something else or come home with us or flee to the nearest watering hole. DO SOMETHING ELSE! Car, windshield. Car, windshield. Christ, no."

From *Rivethead* by Ben Hamper[83]

When autonomous fleets of cabs begin to dominate the roads, the biggest change will be to the number of cars needed to move people around town. If the average car goes from running one hour each day to running ten or fifteen hours in a day, it's possible that the number of cars we need will be reduced by a factor of ten or even more. (See 1.)[110;261]

If we assume that the cars will reach their destination in half the time because they won't stop for traffic lights, we might multiply in another factor of two. (See 11.)

If we assume that the scheduling software will group together people going to similar destinations and similar times, it's possible to imagine that the number of cars needed at rush hour could be cut by a factor of two, three, four or even five. (See 4 and 2.)

If we further note that cabs routinely travel many more miles in their shorter life and avoid the problems associated with old age like rotted rubber hoses, it's possible to estimate that the cars in the future fleet will travel three to four times as far current models. (See 8.)

These are all estimates based on assumptions and it's not fair to simply multiply them together and come to the conclusion that the demand for cars will be cut by a factor of 200 or more but it's clear that all of these effects will all reduce the demand for cars. That means fewer people putting together cars, fewer people making new steel frames, fewer people delivering cars to dealers, fewer people prepping cars for new owners, and just fewer people all along the chain. It's a wonderful vision for anyone who hates steel plants, auto assembly lines and car dealers, but it's a nightmare if you work at one of them. (See 85.)

Of course, not all of these will changes may come to pass. For instance, Brandon Schoettle and Michael Sivak at the University of Michigan Transportation Research Institute assume that people will continue to own their cars and not share them. Even then, they think the average vehicles per household could drop from 2.1 to 1.2 cars.[75;195;196]

There will be new jobs. Cab companies will need to clean their fleet because the riders won't do it any longer. The maintenance crews will check the cars and watch for problems much more often than they do now. The cab companies will need to hire people to do some of the work that the current owners handle, but it's unlikely that these jobs will replace all of the work that people do today to build the millions of cars that sit around for 23+ hours a day.

81

Windows

Cars have had windows from the beginning. The earliest ones
had open cabs and the first enclosed models had windows because the
driver needed to see. Autonomous cars, though, can see with small
cameras and the riders won't have much to do. Windows won't be
essential any longer.

Will people choose autonomous cars with windows? The first ones
will almost certainly have them because it's never good to ask people
to endure too many radical changes. In *The Right Stuff*, Tom Wolfe
described why the early Mercury astronauts insisted that NASA add a
window to the capsule:

> And why? Because *pilots* had windows in their cockpits
> and hatches they could open on their own. That was what
> it was all about: being a *pilot* as opposed to a guinea pig.
> The men hadn't stopped with the window and the hatch,
> either. Not for a moment. Now they wanted ... *manual
> control of the rocket.* They weren't kidding! This was
> to take the form of an override system: if the astronaut
> believed, in his judgment, as captain of the ship (not *cap-
> sule*), that the boost rocket engine was malfunctioning, he
> could take over and guide it himself—- like any proper
> pilot. [252]

The emphasis is Wolfe's but the same holds for the autonomous cars. Early riders aren't going to want to be 'spam in a can', the astronaut's term; they'll want some control over this robot driver and windows are a big part of having a seat at the committee table.

There are certainly some advantages to them. The riders can see where they're going and enjoy the scenery. If they want to change their minds or ask for a quick stop, they'll be able to watch where they are.

But windows also cause trouble. In the summer, they let in too much heat, heat that must be removed by the air conditioner. The fleets will hate this cost and they will probably grow to see windows as an extra expense that breaks too easily and adds too much to the air conditioning bill.

The windows also offer no privacy, letting anyone see in. If the riders really want to see where they're going, they can watch a video feed displayed on a small screen. (A movie thriller will undoubtedly include some plot where the people inside are fooled about their destination with a hacked video feed.)

What will people choose? Today, buses with many passengers have windows so people can watch where they're going but custom coaches designed for smaller groups usually have no windows. Rock and Roll bands on tour almost always have no windows. Limousines usually have blacked out windows that keep outsiders from looking in.

The early riders may want the power of being a captain of a ship, but in time people seem to aspire to the lazy hedonism of being a rock and roll star. They'll probably choose cars with few windows except, perhaps, a small porthole with an opaque shade.

82

Commuting

"Commuting is a migraine-inducing life-suck—a mundane task about as pleasurable as assembling flat-pack furniture or getting your license renewed, and you have to do it *every day*. If you are commuting, you are not spending quality time with your loved ones. You are not exercising, doing challenging work, having sex, petting your dog, or playing with your kids (or your Wii). You are not doing any of the things that make human beings happy. Instead, you are getting nauseous on a bus, jostled on a train, or cut off in traffic."

Annie Lowrey in *Slate*[129]

One of the biggest jobs for a car today is to get the human to a job so the human can afford to feed gas to the car. Commuting is a symbiotic relationship.

Autonomous vehicles will change this game dramatically. Not only will the ride be more efficient (see 14) and less stressful (see 5), but it will be indistinguishable from work itself. Cars with desks and power outlets will let us work to and from the office. The cars will be an office themselves and there will be plenty of work that will be done by people who today are worrying about guiding their cars through traffic. Many workers will get an extra one or two hours to read and type. Some of the heaviest travellers like the sales team will find themselves with many extra hours each week as they ride from stop to stop.[17]

Will we be more productive? Yes, but not as much as it might seem. The background thinking that would normally be done while driving is valuable. Many people need to put an idea aside for a bit and let it come back to them later when they're doing some other light task like driving. If we're more engaged in desk work while riding, we'll have less time for the kind of background contemplation that often unfolds when we're not paying attention. Commuting will rob us of this light dream state that we often enter when traveling along a familiar path.

Commuting will also change because the fleets will be turned into mass transit systems, matching people going to the same destination. (See 44.) It won't always be a moment alone because it will be more practical for people to travel together once the computer matches them with other fellow travellers with similar destinations. Many people who are often forced to ride alone because of the complexity of their trip will be able to find carpools easily.

Despite all of these qualms and complexities, the ability to recapture those hours spent commuting will change life for everyone who is trapped on the road for too long every day. This will be the most important contribution of the invention, the gift of time.

83

Identity

"Well you all may think my story, is more fiction than it's fact. But believe it or not my mother dear decided she'd come back. As a car!"

Theme song to "My Mother the Car" [25]

In 1949, K.C. Douglas and Robert Geddins wrote a song "Mercury Blues" that celebrated the now extinct car brand.

Well if I had money
Tell you what I'd do
I'd go downtown and buy a Mercury or two
Crazy 'bout a Mercury
Lord I'm crazy bout a Mercury [52;64;106]

This wasn't the first song about a brand of cars and it probably won't be the last. This kind of brand identification is something that all companies dream of inspiring and the car companies have been better at it than most companies. Eventually Ford purchased the rights to the song and tweaked it to sell Ford Trucks.

Cars are deeply entwined in our identities. They are among the most expensive things that most people purchase in their lives and so it only makes sense that people make deeper connections with the brands.

Autonomous fleets will change this. It's easy to imagine that the fleets will still try to brand themselves to attract certain groups. Luxurious leather seats, once the hallmark of brands for older car buyers,

185

will also become the hallmark for fleets that are marketing to older riders. The same young, athletic style used to attract buyers to SUVs will be repackaged as a brand to attract younger riders.

The brands won't be focused only on style. Some groups like young parents or older people will have different needs. They'll want cars with doors that open wider for easier entry. If they have babies, they'll want a safer place for them. Other groups will want quieter cars for sleeping. Some will want opulent cars to signal that they can afford something overpriced.

But none of this may come to pass and brands may be largely forgotten because the autonomous cars could destroy the link between the brand and the rider's identity altogether. Does anyone in New York City even bother reading the names of the cab companies on the side of the yellow cars? If the fleets can get riders easily—as they can in New York when it's raining—they won't bother with crafting a style to lure a particular type of rider. If the customers make their decision based upon price and schedule, the style of the car and the extra features may stop mattering. The cars will be just commodities not worthy of song.

84

Status◁

"Deng Xiaoping opened up China's economy with the words 'To get rich is glorious', and the face of China has changed rapidly ever since. Hand in hand with this change has been an infatuation with the automobile and all it symbolizes: wealth, status, and freedom."

review of "The Car that Ate China"[31]

In the later half of the 20th century in America, most aspired to make two major purchases: a house and a car. While both came with many practical benefits, the decisions were soon freighted with many signals about class, ambition and status. Having the right house or car meant something and people spent hours agonizing over which purchase would send the right signal to friends, colleagues and everyone else.

Autonomous car fleets will relegate one of those concerns to history. Everyone will be able to splurge on a wood-paneled, gold-plated model for special occasions and economize with some injection-molded, throwaway cart for everyday commuting. Prices will be negotiable and people will change their ride often.

It's hard to estimate how this will change the market for cars. On one hand, much of the price of a new car goes into features designed to lure buyers. Meticulous grills, chrome highlights and elaborate dashboards are all designed to lure customers who are buying more than a device to get them from here to there. They're also carrying a complicated signal of the owner's status. (See 40 and 7.) Many cab fleets will leave these extras off of their cars and quote lower prices.

On the other hand, more people may choose to pay extra for special occassions or big meetings. Customers who can't afford to purchase an $80,000 car can still afford to pay for one night of the car's life. That could drive up the need for fancier cars.

But this will also change their status. Driving a $200,000 car today shows the world that you can toss around that much money for a car. But paying $200 for 1/1000th of the car's life– perhaps about a day– isn't as impressive. As the public realizes this, the extra value of the status evaporates. People may still rent expensive rides because they love the features, but there will be much less value in proving your wealth and associated status.

85

GDP ◁

> "We're told the gross domestic product (GDP) measures growth, but what it really measures is waste: capital, labor and resources squandered in quixotic pursuit of waste masquerading as 'growth.'
>
> 50 million autos and trucks stuck in traffic, burning millions of gallons of fuel while going nowhere? Growth! All that wasted fuel adds to GDP. Everyone who works from home detracts from 'growth' since they didn't waste fuel sitting in traffic jams.
>
> Repaving a little-used road: growth! Never mind the money could have been invested in repairing a heavily traveled road, or adding safe bikeways, etc.–in the current neo-Keynesian system, building bridges to nowhere is 'growth.'
>
> GDP has no mechanism to measure mal-investment or the opportunity costs of squandering capital, labor and resources on investments with marginal or even negative returns. "

From *GDP = Waste* by Charles Hugh-Smith[98]

Consider this thought experiment: If you follow path A, you buy a shiny new $50,000 car and drive it to a job that pays you $100 per hour. After a year, you collect $200,000 and pay off the car. If you follow path B, you skip that job and choose another paying only $75 per hour that has an office within walking distance of your house. After a year, you collect $150,000.

If there are no taxes in this thought experiment, both paths leave you pretty much with the same amount of cash: $150,000. The Gross Domestic Product (GDP) of the country, though, is dramatically different. You make $50,000 less and, in the eyes of the GDP, do $50,000 less work. There's also one fewer car sold which reduces GDP by about $50,000. This is just the immediate loss. Everyone in the car

189

manufacturing ecosystem will make less money and so they'll spend less at stores, restaurants and other diversions. The affect on GDP of a simple decision like this is not simple to calculate, but it's easy to pump up the number in our imagination. Did walking to work cost the country $1 million, $2 million, or maybe as much as $10 million? Who knows, but in this light it sounds so unpatriotic and selfish. Why are you even reading this cheap book when you could be working harder and spending the extra on a truly lavish and expensive GDP-boosting extravagance?[111]

The economics of an autonomous car fleet are so dramatically different that the shift to robot drivers is bound to change the nation's and the world's GDP and other random statistics. Smart humans may recognize that their lives are getting better, but governments tune the economy by measuring these statistics. Even if they know the measures are problematic[98]– they will need to adapt to the shift and it may not be simple.

Consider the erosion of the car manufacturing business. (See 80.) If a robot cab fleet is truly more efficient, we may end up with a car manufacturing sector that produces 95% fewer units each year. The U.S. government's Department of Commerce estimates that the auto industry employs 3.62 million people and amounted for 3.5% of the GDP. The industry also accounts for $138 billion dollars in exports.[150] It's not unreasonable to imagine that 95% of these jobs, exports and GDP will disappear.

Of course, there will be new jobs and maybe we'll export a few driverless cars, but it's unlikely that these will make much of a dent. The stats will be permanently gone, along with the GDP that was once filled by horse farriers, blacksmiths, buggy manufacturers and saddle stitchers.

The car business is not as large a part of the economy as it was in the past, but it is still significant. Some parts of the U.S. government work hard to ensure that the GDP grows by 1-2% a year. A quick rollout of autonomous cars could lead to a dip in the GDP and a statistical recession as the lack of earnings filter through the economy.

And what about the bankers who need the car loans (see 56), the mechanics (see 8), the billboard crews (see 72) etc.?

Chunka Mui at Forbes thinks the numbers may be much larger, perhaps several trillion of disruption. He doesn't limit the ripple effects to the auto industry but includes others like gasoline and emergency rooms at hospitals that will have many fewer jobs doing reconstructive surgery as car crashes diminish.[139;140] (See 65.) But is it accurate to say that several hundred billion or even several trillion dollars of wealth will just go "Poof"? When the rollout begins, Americans will graduate from being working class shleps who drove themselves into the ranks of the rich who ride in limousines and spend their auto dollars elsewhere. GDP may shrink but everyone will start living like kings. Numbers will fail us. And statistics like GDP won't capture how wonderful our lives may become.

This wouldn't be so bad if the numbers were just numbers, flashing on some screen. But economic numbers have consequences because the government tries to regulate the economy. They want the GDP to grow because that generally means more jobs and more jobs generally means more happiness– no matter what people say at 7am in the morning on their way to work. And let's not forget that more jobs mean more taxes. If the numbers crash, the government may try to regulate their way to creating more GDP and bringing the needle on the GDP dashboard back where it's thought to belong. That could be even more disruptive than the robot cars themselves.

86

Immigration◁

> "This analysis tests the often-made argument that immigrants only do jobs Americans don't want. If the argument is correct, there should be occupations comprised entirely or almost entirely of immigrants. But Census Bureau data collected from 2005 to 2007, which allow for very detailed analysis, show that even before the recession there were only a tiny number of majority-immigrant occupations."

Steven A. Camarota and Karen Zeigler [23]

It's no secret that in the United States the legacy cab business was a favorite of recent immigrants looking for jobs. Low wages and a lack of discrimination meant that people often looked for work in cab driving when they arrived in America.

Not all countries have this pattern. England, for instance, uses rigorous exams about London's streets to turn cab driving into a serious profession. Drivers often spend months studying to take the test. Alas, the arrival of navigation apps has undercut all of that hard work and made their knowledge vestigial.

The competition from robot drivers will have the same effect on drivers. There will be one fewer industry willing to hire immigrants, something that may deter more from coming to America.

Of course, it could also have the opposite effect if robot cars kill jobs around the world. More unemployed people mean more people willing to migrate in search of work.

87

Delivery

> "I was recently traveling on Singapore Air (although not through Singapore), and I was thinking about Singapore's death to drug smugglers laws. I wondered if there has been a case where someone with extremely malicious intent planted some contraband on an innocent traveler to Singapore. It would seem like a very clever (and evil, of course) way of rubbing out one's enemy. Not that I'm planning on doing this..."
>
> Internet discussion about airport security [48]

Every day, the Post Office, Fed Ex, UPS and a few more send trucks down my street with packages for people. If the autonomous cars can carry people, why can't they carry things? They will, although it won't be as easy for the autonomous cars to replace the driver of the package delivery truck.

The fleet of cars can pick up packages just like people. The cars can stop by grocery stores, warehouses or people's houses when someone calls for a delivery. The shipper can make a reservation for a package just like a rider can make one for a person. In all of these cases, it's likely that a person will be handy to load the package into the back of the car. The car picking up the package will be programmed to arrive at a convenient time for the shipper.

The other end of the journey will be a bit more confusing. The mail carriers and package delivery teams walk up stairs, across lawns and around many obstacles that cars can't handle. While it's conceivable that the cars could simply sport some spring-loaded arm that can toss the packages toward the house, it would only work for simpler items

195

like a newspaper. The current infrastructure, alas, may be easily adaptable for autonomous vehicles, but not for autonomous delivery. It will be several years before robots can do what human postal carriers do every day.

The bushes, ruts and door bells aren't the only hurdles. Human delivery networks are plagued by theft. Thieves tail delivery trucks and wait for them to leave a package on a door stop. A few minutes later, the thieves walk up to the front door and take the package.[95;199] In many cases, the delivery companies aren't very forthcoming with reimbursements because that would only open them up to a different kind of fraud.

One simple but more expensive solution would be to require the recipient to walk out to the road to accept the package from the back of the car. When the package travel is being booked, the recipient could commit to a delivery time and the car could hold it in the trunk until it was convenient for both the car and the recipient. This is, however, much more of a hassle than we're used to with the current system.

Delivering goods with the fleet is bound to save a dramatic amount of energy and reduce the amount of greenhouse gases added to the atmosphere. One study by Erica Wygonik and Anne Goodchild[255] examined how people could cut back fuel use and CO_2 emissions by more than 90% by switching to a grocery delivery service that used an optimized route. Selecting the groceries at home and letting the fleet deliver them is much more efficient than taking a personal trip.

Autonomous vehicles will be more vulnerable to theft because the cars won't be able to defend the goods, aside from perhaps announcing in a computer-generated voice, "Stop! Thief!" Humans are territorial and they often respect the zones defined by other humans. People shoplift less when other humans are around. These robot delivery agents won't be able to count on what intraspecies respect exists.

Some companies imagine better places for delivery appearing on houses and businesses. Amazon wants to put lockers in stores like Staples.[13;164] The stores will get more foot traffic in return for holding packages for people. The company is already testing the system in Washington.

The grocery delivery chains dream of refrigerated delivery boxes outside houses much like the coolers used by milk men long ago. The house where my great grandmother lived in New Jersey had a small delivery chamber in a wall with doors on the inside and the outside.

Homes could easily add these lockable storage compartments.

It won't be simple, but if these lockers are designed carefully, they could accept packages from autonomous cars. The car companies could create design guidelines not unlike the ones imposed by the post office on mailboxes. People who wanted the convenience would build larger mailboxes near the road that the autonomous cars could easily reach.

The lockers may even be designed as moveable trailers to be dropped off full and picked up when empty. There will be a demand for trailers to carry personal items that people won't want to load and unload each day. These pods or personal trailers could also serve a big role in the delivery network. (See 77 and 79.)

88

Tourism

"In rural area of Japan, you can find 'Michi no Eki' (means Road Station) where you can park and rest 24h. I sometimes sleep in my sleeping bag in my car. This practice is called 'Shachu haku'."

from `japan-guide.com`.

When we would drive by the hospital where I was born, my mother would tell us who was born there. When we drive by a house where my wife's grandfather lived, she tells our children about him. Looking out the window is like going to a museum of the world and it's better with a tour guide.

The autonomous car will change tourism. Not only will our cars be able to offer a tape loop description of the most important buildings and locations of interest to everyone, but they'll also be able to customize this information stream in innumerable ways. If we're willing to share our calendars, our Facebook feeds and the list of articles we've read, the cars will be able to point out interesting details as we roll along. (See 54.)

It would be possible to cross-correlate the genealogical records with the tax records to point out every house where your no-good uncles and saintly great-grandmother lived. The car will know where your friends ate dinner four years ago and it will be able to tell you what they tweeted about in the neighborhood where you're driving. More and more photos, emails, comments and whatnot will be geotagged and all of that information will be ripe for the indefatigable wit of the autonomous tour guide. Some of the information will appear on heads-up displays painted on the windows (if they exist, see 81) and others will just appear in a non-stop verbal narrative from a chatty autonomous cab driver.

"Excuse me sir, you know that story about the world's largest pancake that you read about 832.2 days ago?" the car might interrupt. "It was 17 days after your birthday? You must remember it. If you turn to your right, you'll see the restaurant where it was cooked. Your friend Harry only gave it 2 stars but your friend Megan gave it 5+++ stars. Did I mention that she gives this ranking to more than 86% of the restaurants that she reviews? Sorry, she gave your new book only 4 stars on Amazon."

89

Policing

> "It was terribly dangerous to let your thoughts wander when you were in any public place or within range of a telescreen. The smallest thing could give you away. A nervous tic, an unconscious look of anxiety, a habit of muttering to yourself —anything that carried with it the suggestion of abnormality, of having something to hide. In any case, to wear an improper expression on your face (to look incredulous when a victory was announced, for example) was itself a punishable offense. There was even a word for it in Newspeak: facecrime, it was called. "
>
> George Orwell in *1984* [16]

Every viewer of a crime drama knows that electronic devices are snitches. The police regularly retrieve data from computers and mobile phones that help them solve cases, and only a fool would believe that the autonomous vehicle will offer much privacy. (See 52.) If the cars are just rented, their owners will probably install some kind of video cameras to stop vandalism. The information from those cameras and all of the fleet's computers will be readily available and used to indict riders who break the law.

A deeper question is whether the autonomous fleets will do more than just track the riders themselves. The cars will be roaming the cities and the cars will be loaded with cameras that are guiding the car. They can also be recording this data and maybe doing even more. One gigabyte can store one hour of very high quality video and a two-terabyte drive can hold 2,000 camera hours. A car with ten cameras would still carry the last eight days or so on one disk. They'll be like roving security cameras. If the fleets are big enough, they'll have a detailed record of the city. They won't be perfectly distributed and they'll miss many events, but they'll tend to be near where the people happen to be.

The cars will also have the computer power to do more than just record the video. Facial recognition algorithms are cheap to run and so the car can pre-index the video with the faces of everyone it passes. It's just a few extra cycles of computer time but it could produce a database with unprecedented scope.

The cameras aren't the only sensors. Many car tires have RFID chips in them and the car could note the responses from every tire that passes close by. Cell phone signals and Bluetooth chips will uniquely identify all of the mobile handsets near the car. Indeed, our current generation of handsets can be compiling this information already.

The data doesn't need to be used to prosecute people. The mobile platforms can be recording any kind of data about the environment like the humidity or air quality. (See 93.)

An interesting distinction will emerge between the car owners and the car renters. Many people from across the financial spectrum will love the simplicity of renting rides, but the economics will generally mean that it will just be too expensive for most people to consider owning. Only the car lovers will make the sacrifice just as only people who love to fly their own planes continue to pay the high costs of owning a Cessna.

This will lead to a difference in freedom and privacy. The car owners will still own the data about them because they control the platform, the car, and the data it generates. The renters, though, will give up their data to the fleet owner who will be free to do what they want with it. In other words, only the car *owners* will maintain their fourth amendment rights to the data on their movements.

90

Road Maintenance

"Michigan doesn't need welcome signs to alert travelers they've crossed our border; they can feel it in their teeth. Molar-jarring potholes pock our roads and let interstate motorists know, 'You're not in Ohio anymore.'"

Leslie Macmillian, *New York Times*[234]

Wouldn't it be neat to have a button on the dashboard that would allow you to report a pothole whenever you discover one while driving? There are already a number of smartphone apps for reporting problems and there are some that are even trying to use the accelerometer to detect potholes.[50;115;137;244] The devices are creating vast databases about what needs to be fixed.

The autonomous vehicles will take the human out of the loop in road maintenance, too, because they'll have the ability to monitor the road as they roll along and report any problem. They will be rolling robot quality assurance inspectors who will be able to call up their robot maintenance supervisors to fix something ASAP. And if we have autonomous cars, then autonomous road maintenance crews can't be far behind. This might even be made a bit easier if the roads are replaced with thin concrete paths like railroads. The autonomous maintenance robots will be able to swap out bad ones with good ones with little human intervention.

The roads are just the beginning. The cars will be loaded with cameras and they'll be able to analyze everything they see. Just as they can detect and report human problems (see 89), they will be able to notice many problems with a city's physical plant. Graffiti, for instance, can

203

be detected quickly by comparing the current video feed with the one from a few days before. If the mark is removed quickly, the graffiti artists lose the notoriety, become discouraged and move on to other hobbies.

Many cities also spend heavily on sending inspectors to watch bridges and other road beds. While much of this work requires smart humans to peek beneath the surface, the cars can still identify new cracks and other visible problems. They may even be sensitive to detect different vibrational changes in the road bed. If the supports are weakening or something is about to give way, the resonant patterns of the roads may shift. The autonomous vehicles can be gathering constant data about the way that the road bed responds to the cars and this can be compared to the historical record. Some careful statistical analysis, although not perfect, will offer the potential of detecting problems before they become serious.

91

Owning the Roads◁

Singing Wind We always thought bead was worthless. We assumed our ancestors were cheated because they not have concept of ownership.
Bender So we can have the diamond?
Singing Wind No, we do have concept of ownership.

From "Futurama"[79]

Many early long-distance roads were owned by private companies who paid to build them and recouped their investment through tolls. Governments now build most roads. Local roads are free and largely maintained by taxes while highways are supported by a mixture of tolls and taxes. All of this money flows through local and state governments.

This model of common ownership has many advantages. Everyone is free to use the roads as they need allowing for innovation, experimentation and exploration with few limits. Tax revenue often comes from sales of gasoline, a proxy for road usage that is under strain. More and more states and local governments are complaining about the appearance of electric and hybrid cars as well as highly fuel-efficient vehicles that some say aren't paying their "fair share."

Large, centralized fleets of autonomous vehicles cars could open the door to private ownership of roads. Railroads, for instance, have always bundled together real estate and rolling stock. If they don't own the land and the rails outright, they pay directly for using the right-of-way. They usually handle maintenance themselves, although in some cases the tracks are owned by the government.

Allowing more private ownership may accelerate the transition because private entities are often better at driving change than centralized governments. Autonomous fleets promise to produce an enormous stream of data about where the public wants to go and when it wants to get there. If there's heavy demand, roads can be expanded and if there's little demand, they can shrink, perhaps to as small as two thin strips set to the width of the tires. (See 34.)

In many ways, the question is not about ownership per se. A successful partnership between a private, profit-seeking company and the government can ensure that a substantial amount of the savings from maintenance can be returned to the public coffers. Plunder will always be an issue, but private ownership can spur development by making the difficult decisions more quickly than the public sector. While there will be many who dislike the decisions, they won't have the same power to thwart change as they do in the many layers of traditional government. Asking every community board to have power over the shape of the roads may be too much.

92

Construction

"Riggs climbs up through a car's sunroof and then onto the back of a vehicle transporting a modular home to get at some bad guys.... Riggs fights with a thug inside a modular home (on a moving truck) with many punches and kicks. After coming close to doing so several times, they end up falling through the plastic sheeting on one side and the thug is graphically hit by a truck. Riggs then holds on as he 'freeway skis' behind the first truck on a table atop the plastic sheet while another thug tries to run him over with a car. Murtaugh then bangs his car into the thug's and the two continue to smash into each other's cars."

ScreenIt.com review warning parents about what children might imitate from "Lethal Weapon 4" [229]

Shipping a large object down a road today requires multiple permits, special trucks and extra escorts with big signs warning "Wide Load" even though the load is usually so big that everyone sees the load before the sign. In the future, the reservation system will allow people to reserve roads by the foot making it possible to book a path that's two or three lanes wide.

Big objects will be easier to move. Big construction equipment will move more easily through the world and not require all of the extra care it takes today. Cranes and earthmoving machines will travel quickly to where they are needed before moving on.

More construction will move into factories where construction is faster and more precise. Some companies already build homes in sections that are one lane wide and then bolt them together when they arrive at the site. Factories will be able to create double and triple wide

207

mobile homes that move in one piece. This may make it possible to create entire homes and drive them to their location in one piece.

Construction won't be the only industry to benefit. Many others will gain flexibility and freedom with the ability to ship machinery and goods in larger sections. It won't just be people who enjoy the freedom of the roads, but things too.

93

Weather

"Your honor, the plaintiff claims that it was because of Chief Thundercloud's rain dance that it rained. I claim that it was the act of washing the car that caused it to rain. Everybody knows, that the minute you wash your car, it rains!"

From "Green Acres" [212]

The cars can gather more than just information about criminals (see 89) or pot holes (see 90); they can be gathering information about the entire city. The U.S.Postal Service, for instance, is investigating mounting sensor pods on their delivery vehicles and using them to study the environment, the weather, pollution and anything that might need widespread data gathering. Their fleet already moves through almost every American neighborhood on five or six days each week. [49;174]

A fleet of autonomous cars will be even more ubiquitous. Wherever people live and work, the cars will go. They'll travel the roads more often at all hours that humans move.

A simple system of networks can gather even better weather data than we currently have. It can monitor temperature and barometric changes and produce the most accurate data about microclimates that we've ever had. This can be turned into even more accurate weather forecasts and also allow us to understand just how climate differs in the same regions.

The cars will even be able to use this information to take better care of themselves. They'll be able to anticipate when rain or sleet will make the roads a bit slippery and they'll slow down. They'll also be able to report icy patches when their tires lose their grip allowing the network to dispatch salt trucks. They may even know when they'll need a bath and arrange to drive to the rainy part of town when the skies open up. They'll be able to clean themselves with a free car wash.

94

Snow and Rain

"**Driving backwards on an icy road is safer than driving forward because of improved traction.—BUSTED** Although it was found that cars can achieve better traction on an icy road while driving in reverse, the increased traction didn't offset the sheer difficulty of driving in reverse. Each member of the Build Team drove a different type of vehicle through an icy course and each of them had more difficulty completing the course in reverse than while driving forward."

Summary of Mythbusters research on driving in snow [101]

Just as it rains on the just and the unjust, snow and rain will make life difficult for autonomous cars just like cars driven by humans. The stuff just makes the roads slipperier. Computers may be able to do many things better than humans, but it's not clear that they can do much about the coefficient of friction between tires and an icy road.

But there are still opportunities that smart fleets can exploit. First, computers don't panic like humans. They can learn to steer into a spin and apply brakes in just the right pattern to avoid locking them. We already rely upon the little computer in anti-lock brakes to do that for us humans. The autonomous cars will be even smarter and better at it.

The smart cars will also be able to communicate and share information with others. (See 93.) If a section of the road is icy, they can tell others who will learn from the mistakes of the cars that went before them. Humans have trouble doing that unless the fishtailing car is right in front of them.

The smart fleets can slow down and offer slower quoted travel times when people try to reserve a trip. This will usually lead to higher prices when the weather is bad just because more car time is needed.

The price can also rise to reflect the higher risk, essentially incorporating the increased danger into the price as a form of insurance. (See 26.) This flexibility will allow fleets to signal that it's safer to just stay home. After all, if autonomous cars crash, the weather will still be cold and help may not arrive in time.

Autonomous cars may also take part in road maintenance. Many cities spray brine or beet juice on the roads before a major snowstorm, essentially pre-salting them. The autonomous fleets can be fitted with these spray tanks and they can follow the instructions of a central computer. There won't be a need for an extra salt truck.

It may be possible for the autonomous cars to do some of the plowing. While larger snowfalls will require heftier trucks with bigger engines, lightweight cars can plow several inches of snow. If the entire fleet is outfitted with the plows, they can scrape the roads during the storm while carrying passengers or freight. If a car with a snowplow is sent down a street every hour or two, it will only need to push off an inch or two even during the heaviest storms. Repeated plowing can be more efficient if the cars are doing a double or triple duty by carrying people and packages.

The autonomous fleets may choose to simply ignore the snow and skip plowing it. Many cities and counties in rural areas don't plow the roads very often during the storm and they just require the cars to have chains. It's easier for fleets to add chains or other hefty tires to their cars during the winter, in part because they will be swapping off tires much more often than the average family car today. Some fleet cars could easily travel 10,000 to 20,000 during a month, wearing out tires every few months. These fleets could add good snow tires in the winter and optimize driving when the snow falls.

95

Highways

"A particularly dramatic case in point comes to us from traffic-clogged Seoul, Korea, where a few years ago a handful of 'crazy' visionaries in the transport department somehow managed to sell a new mayor on the demolition of an elevated downtown highway. Fast-forward to today: the highway's gone, a formerly paved-over river has been rehabilitated, the resulting green space is a source of urban pride, and—wait for it—motor vehicle travel times have actually improved in the neighborhood of the old highway."

Chris Turner in *Mother Nature Network* [161;172;225]

The main reason that freeways, highways, parkways, thruways, and turnpikes exist is because starting and stopping a car is so time-consuming and energy-wasting. All of that energy spent getting up to speed is turned into heat when we push down on the brakes. Even hybrids fail to capture all of the energy during braking.

But what happens if the stoplights can be timed so that few cars even stop at the corners? (See 11.) If the timing can be worked out, cars will be able to maintain speeds of 40 to 50 miles per hour in the city grid. I already see people moving 30 to 40 m.p.h. on the city streets with street lights timed with current techniques. Better, faster timing will make it possible for the grid to support freeway speed timing.

Will we still want to keep the freeways? They cost plenty of money to build, and removing them will cost money too, but many cities are finding that it's worth it to replace elevated freeways with ground-level boulevards. The grand, new roads become centerpieces with higher real estate values and beautiful views.

San Francisco, for instance, removed its freeway along the Embarcadero after the 1989 Loma Prieta earthquake damaged it. A number of activists and urban planners wanted to destroy it before the earthquake, but inertia prevented them from gathering the votes and the money. The earthquake made repair too expensive. Today the road is lined with beautiful parks and shops and the waterfront is in much greater demand. Bringing the cars to ground level encouraged the investment in the shops alongside the road because no one liked the view below the freeway.[56;117;204]

The most interesting detail is that travel is still relatively fast. The city is able to time the lights to balance the flow from the boulevard to the adjacent streets. The traffic doesn't race down the freeway only to back up near the exit ramps. Other cities are reporting similar success with removing big, elevated freeways.

The sophisticated timing algorithms available for autonomous cars will make it even easier to redesign the cityscapes and bring back the dense urban designs that encourage walking and interaction but with better traffic flow. The ground-level grid will be able to deliver both.

96

Emergency Vehicles

"A pregnant woman en route to the hospital gave birth Wednesday morning in an unexpected spot: a traffic jam in west suburban Cicero. ... Contractions came faster and faster, and the couple pulled into a nearby gas station parking lot where Katie Morales delivered baby Aidan in their van around 8 a.m. "

Lisa Balde and Anthony Ponce, NBC Chicago[8]

In 1986, paramedics in midtown Manhattan started using tiny cars that can drive along the sidewalks because the roads were too jammed for ambulances to move quickly. The problem has gotten so bad that some have even suggested banning larger sport utility vehicles from the city simply to make it easier for ambulances to get where they need to go.[96;216]

Autonomous cars won't have to listen for a siren, but will be able to monitor a central emergency channel and move out of the way when an ambulance, fire truck or police car needs to get through. And they will only need to get out of the way on the side of the street on which the ambulance is traveling, letting the other side flow freely.

Routing algorithms can also guide emergency vehicles around road blocks or other problems that prevent cars from getting out of the way, finding the clearest path for emergency vehicles. This will be even more valuable when large disasters make evacuation essential. (See 97.)

97

Evacuation◁

"If we faced a countdown to destruction, could we build a spacecraft to take us to new and habitable worlds? Can we Evacuate Earth? This documentary special examines this terrifying but scientifically plausible scenario by exploring how we could unite to ensure the survival of the human race."

From "Evacuate Earth". [194]

When disaster strikes, people flea. Some of the most forward-thinking cities and states have disaster plans for making it easier. The Outer Banks of North Carolina, for instance, have been threatened by hurricanes so often during the August vacation season that they have a special plan for getting people off the island. [14;232;238] And they are not alone. Most coastal regions have similar plans to evacuate residents and visitors ahead of approaching storms.

A large fleet of autonomous cars run by a central planning system could enhance and speed evacuation efforts during emergencies. Local transportation could be canceled to give priority to evacuating cars. Lanes directions could also be changed so most or even all lanes on major arteries are carrying people out of harm's way.

The system can even be arranged to activate temporary roads or seldom-used paths and put them into service. Cities may create special emergency roads through parks or other areas that are only used when disaster makes them essential. Such temporary or overflow paths could dramatically increase the amount of traffic able to flow from a region. (See 34.)

But there will also be potential downsides. In many areas of the

United States, there are enough cars to carry many of the people. The autonomous car revolution, however, will be pushed by the low cost of fleets of cars. If some of the predictions are correct (see 80), the emerging fleet could only have the capacity to move as little as 2-10% at one time. Saving money by eliminating little used cars rusting in driveways will also mean that we may not have a large enough fleet available to move people in a disaster.

Not all areas, though, have such a surplus of cars. Many of the largest cities are already filled with people who don't own cars. Evacuating New York, for instance, is practically impossible because so few own cars and public transit can't handle such a surge. Many poor areas in all regions are also carless. For them, the argument is moot.

One solution is to send robot cars back into the region to pick up more people. This will be practical and even emotionally simple because it won't require sending humans back into danger but it will require that almost an equal number of lanes be directed into the area. It won't be easy to simply redirect all lanes out of town because the cars will need to return to pick up more.

There will also be a lack of capacity to move essential items. There will be fewer trucks and cars with trunks ready to carry anything that people want to move out of harm's way. If a large fraction of the future autonomous fleet is dedicated to cars for morning commuters with one seat and little or no cargo space, then it will be difficult to evacuate cargo too.

However, nearby regions can redirect some of their fleet to the emergency area. One region would sacrifice the ability to move about so others in danger can flee. This could create a much larger fleet that could move more people out faster than before. Some large cities with few cars like New York could easily become more mobile in the face of danger after the autonomous cars arrive.

98

Airports

"In a moment, we watch him running through an airport, attaching and detaching various bombs, hurriedly scurrying onto the back of a truck, leaping into a plane and shooting into the sky, delayed by another plane's explosion, but making it through all the same. As I watched, I knew that I was going to get what I had been promised—explosive action, gorgeous women, and lots of fun."

Max Scheinin, review of "Tomorrow Never Dies" [190]

Autonomous cars will remake the air travel business by handling longer overnight hauls that deliver the rider rested and ready (see 76) and, perhaps, sprouting wings (see 99), but they will also reshape the architecture of the old monstrosity, the airport.

The modern airport is a marvelous creation of mandatory ticket fees and oversized construction budgets. Broad corridors and soaring hallways let passengers walk for miles to get to their gate. Huge security paddocks take long enough to traverse that passengers often must arrive hours before their flight, allowing them plenty of time to shop in the mall on the other side. If only they didn't have to lug their purchases on their trip, shop owners would have a perfect captive audience.

Autonomous vehicles will make most of this concrete obsolete. Huge parking towers will be left empty when autonomous cabs start carrying people to the airport. Many people already take cabs or vans because of onerous parking fees. When autonomous vehicles drive down prices, the only parking spaces necessary will be for the buffer of cars waiting for the next batch of planes to arrive.

The steady stream of autonomous cars will eliminate the need for five-lane passages where three or even four lanes are clogged with double, triple and sometimes quadruple-parked cars picking up or dropping off passengers.

A smart solution would be to let the cabs drive through the broad corridors and drop off the passengers directly at the gate but that will only last until we demolish the old terminals. Autonomous cars will be able to meet planes on the tarmac like in "Casablanca" and save the cost of heating and cooling the huge corridors altogether. Future airports might just be a loop with gates that are pull offs where autonomous cars drop off passengers at small huts to keep them warm or cool for a few minutes as they wait.

Perhaps the planes may even load the pods or cars and fly them from spot to spot and the passengers won't get out—something that might only work if the transport is light enough. Why waste the energy flying the extra hardware around?

If the cars are able to deliver their passengers with any accuracy, there won't be a need for any building at all. Passengers will get out of the car, walk through a security scanner and bound up the steps to the plane. Scheduling algorithms can assign passengers thin slots of time for transferring from car to plane and the cars will deliver them just in time. The airplane will be merely another link in the mass transit system. (See 44.)

A central terminal will still be needed to hold the passengers changing planes, but this won't need to be very big. A local fleet of cabs will carry passengers from gate to terminal and on to the next gate.

Computer algorithms will choose the best combinations and it may end up that people will take flights that travel to different cities than their intended destination and complete the journey with a longer car ride. Optimizing algorithms could juggle everything, including adding and subtracting charter flights for particular events. The same algorithms that will remake the car business will allow airlines to add and subtract flights easily when special events, games or conventions drive up demand to get to certain locations. Many of the ideas from this book also apply to the airline business, which can customize its routes with the same portals.

99

Flying Cars

"Hi friends, Goldie Wilson III for Wilson Hover Conversion Systems. You know, when my Grandpa was Mayor of Hill Valley, he had to worry about traffic problems. But now, you don't have to worry about traffic. I'll hover convert your old road car into a skyway flyer! For only $39,999.95. So come on down and see me, Goldie Wilson III, at any one of our 29 convenient locations. Remember, keep 'em flying!"

TV commercial embedded in "Back to the Future 2" [259]

The flying car is one of the great clichés of the future. For years, people have been predicting that flying cars are going to be coming soon and yet they never appear overhead.

Dismissing them, though, as a failed prediction is not really fair. There have been several flying cars on the market and none ever became more than a gimmick. One of the first, the Aerocar, started production in 1946 but never attracted more than a few handfuls of buyers. [178]

Many dreamers continue to feel a bit sad about this because there are many practical reasons why flying cars would make our lives easier. There is so much space to maneuver in three dimensions that we can usually take the shortest path between places. (One of my friends once tried to fly over Camp David when the president was vacationing there and he was met by Secret Service agents when he landed.) While planes need to worry about traffic near airports, the odds of even coming close to each other is low in regular flight. Flying cars would eliminate much of the complexity of routing algorithms for getting from place to place by letting us leave the troubles of earth behind us when we take off.

Flying is also getting easier than ever. The widespread use of GPS devices and better designed planes makes it simpler than ever. Autonomous flying drones are common and they are easier to build than the autonomous cars that must navigate around people, curbs and all of the hassles of Earth. People are already building autonomous drones in their basements, and it wouldn't be hard to create drones that carry people.

Despite these temptations, there are plenty of practical reasons why the flying cars are not common. While flying can be faster, that makes it significantly less fuel efficient.

The Aerocar had an anemic engine driving the wheels and it could only make 60mph on the ground. When it was flying, the rear pusher prop needed to get the car up to 110mph in order for the wings to generate enough lift.

This difference is significant because the amount of power to push a car through the air is often related to the **cube** of the velocity. Doubling the speed will increase the amount of power required by a factor of 8. That means a larger engine and more fuel. This same rule also affects cars near the ground although the computations are a bit complex. Anyone who wants to go faster will need to pay attention. [1]

There are wings that work at slower speeds, and some flying car-like devices poke along at 50-60mph. While they don't suffer from the high cost of overcoming drag, they still are much less efficient because they often require two different engines or transmissions, one for the wheels and one for the prop. That drives up the cost and adds extra weight that's expensive to get off the ground.

This doesn't stop people from dreaming. One new company called Terrafugia is testing a new model that they plan to sell for $279,000. It's coming soon and it will have an autopilot that does most of the piloting in the air. Now it just needs a similar tool for the ground. [43;92;162]

---

[1] Daniel Gross notes in an article in *Slate* that flying has gotten more energy efficient than driving over the years, but this is largely because the airplanes are packed with hundreds of people while the utilization rate for cars is dropping as fewer share rides. [81]

Transition

Scientists can build self-driving cars. They have been proven safe in limited tests. Plenty of people want them. So, how do we get from here to there? [11;87;226]

There are a number of paths:

One Big Rollout A manufacturer could start selling the cars. They are legal in California and Nevada as long as the driver stands ready. There are plenty of people in those states who would be willing to pay for the novelty, even if they had to sit alert in the driver's seat. There would be a price premium at first, but it could decline quickly. Putting autonomous cars in the hands of individuals wouldn't be the same as building a cab fleet, but it would fit with current laws.

Human Backup The cars could do everything but the human could always take charge. California, for instance, is requiring Google's test cars to maintain a steering wheel that humans could use to take charge. [3;103;113] This would make it easier for people to trust the machines but it might not offer the safety that people imagine. If the riders aren't regularly in charge of the vehicle, they will probably let their mind drift and take up other tasks like using a cell phone. They won't necessarily see the danger in time to take control.

Remote Assistance The person taking over does not need to be in the car itself. If an unforseen situation appears or the computer becomes confused, it can pass over control to several professional human drivers in an emergency center. They would be able to take over control of any vehicle. By doing this daily, they would also keep their driving skill fresh– a big advantage over the basic riders who would start to let their abilities atrophy the more they ride.

Cab Rollout Someone could purchase a cab fleet in a progressive city starved for mass transit. The fleet could book rides via smartphone and limit the trips to those within a well-tested area. In time, the area could expand as people become more comfortable.

Open Source Google gave away its Android operating system successfully, allowing the company to place its search tool in the hands of millions of users. Google could follow the same path with its car-driving software. The company would make money from ad revenue and let manufacturers decide how to add software to their cars. The Android phone market is vibrant and full of experimentation, but it is not lucrative for Google. This approach may allow them to avoid some of the liability issues but it would push them onto someone else's back.

Experimental Hobbyists A substantial fraction of the small planes built in the United States are kits assembled by the owner, a legal dodge that allows kit manufacturers to avoid liability. A few small companies could start offering aftermarket enhancements for cars that provide some or all of the navigation features. There would be little coherent regulation because the installations would be done by people in their garages who would turn on autonomous guidance whenever they feel like it. Given the fraction of cars with illegal window tinting, illegal mufflers, and other aftermarket infractions, it is not hard to imagine how autonomous vehicles could slowly fill the highways.

Drone Piloting Self-driving cars available today don't need much help, but if they do, they could pull over to the side of the road and start a wireless link to a central command center staffed with drivers who would remotely drive the car back to a place where the computer could take control again. This central command could be staffed with a few humans who could help ease the qualms that a human is not in charge.

Gradual New Features Major car companies are already adding more and more automation. Some cars can park themselves.

Others can follow lane markers on major highways. Some can stop quickly if the car in front of them stops. These features are slowly taking more and more control away from the driver and someday they could converge to create a completely autonomous unit. This gradual introduction of new features won't scare anyone and will allow major companies to slowly adapt without losing the market. The hidden danger is that as drivers get more and more bored with their diminished responsibilities, they'll stop concentrating and there will be more crashes as they fail to remain alert for the remaining items that the technology isn't able to handle .

Lawyers and Unions Win Opponents also could succeed in stopping them. Plenty of jobs that might be disrupted by the new technology and established stakeholders can be expected to play every card to maintain control and keep their jobs. Cab drivers could demonize the computer-controlled automobile. Car makers could push for more regulation. Lawyers may target software companies, who could flee to other nations that would leapfrog America.

Fast Forward

One of the questions I like to ask people at parties is whether their kids will ever get drivers' licenses. My children are 12 and 10 as I write this and I've been asking the question of everyone, but mainly of parents with kids about the same age. The response is always, "Yes!" and it usually comes with squinting eyes and look of suspicion because it sounds like a trick question. They seem to wonder where it was going. Did it hold a veiled jab, perhaps an implication that their kid wasn't smart enough to handle the road? Did I know something about their kids that they didn't?

The question seems confusing even though it's not. No one wants to consider that self-driving cars are coming faster than we think. A lawyer I know who helps keeps the Lincoln Town Car brand in business by hiring chauffeur-driven rides, believes it will never happen. The cars would never arrive. Not in his lifetime and not in mine. When I explained that some autonomous cars had already driven hundreds of thousands of miles without an accident, he wouldn't budge. When I pointed out that California and Nevada had already made the cars legal, he still wouldn't budge.

When will they arrive? That's not the right question because they're already here. The right one to ask is when will you and I be able to punch up an app on our phone and book a ride somewhere.

This book has made a number of predictions and as Yogi Berra pointed out, predictions are tough, especially about the future. I'm sure that most of the changes will come true in some shape or form, but I'm also sure that some will fall short. How far short? I won't even guess.

Consider the question of how many cars will be left on the road after a number of these changes take effect. Fleets of cabs (see 1) could easily do the work of ten cars with just one cab. More efficient intersections (see 11) and central planning could speed the grid by a factor of two or more. Flexible carpools and ad hoc bus routes (see 44 and 4) could easily toss in another factor of two or more. Things don't look good for parking garages (see 32) or people on assembly lines (see 80).

But other effects may change the car ecosystem. If the price of travel drops precipitously, people may take more trips. If they can work (see 82) or sleep (see 76) in their cars, they may want to go farther and that will increase the number of miles driven each year.

All of this will affect prices in uncertain ways. Costs will get lower as fleets deploy more efficient cars that live longer, exploit better route planning (see 44) and access to alternative fuels. (See 27.) The price of getting from here to there is bound to drop.

Or will it? Fewer cars on the road mean fewer chances to amortize all of the design costs (see 80). But then maybe design won't be as important because people will just be booking a ride, not investing in a lifestyle and so the cab companies will use the same design forever like Checker did. Or maybe it will be because people will crave novelty in their ride in the same way that they search it out in restaurants and so cab companies will need to create ever stranger coaches to carry their jaded customers (see 77).

Along the way, society will change and adapt to the new autonomous cars. Perhaps even more people will flock to cities because density makes everything more convenient (see 30). And fast, stable cab systems will make city life better for everyone. Or perhaps everyone will decide that owning their own mansion in the middle of nowhere is what they want because travel is so much easier and they'll book twice as many miles in the cars (see 38). I can't be certain about the details, but it's clear that change will come.

Will all of this unfold quickly enough to save our children or grandchildren from driving? I tried telling the lawyer that the iPhone went from impossibly cool to almost passé in five years but he wouldn't budge. Wouldn't happen, he said as he stood his ground.

Despite all of these facts, he couldn't see that the rest of the world was just like him. Everyone wants to ride in a Lincoln Town Car with a chauffeur and that alone would be enough to overcome all of the obstacles. That desire to live like a big shot lawyer with a driver on call will provide enough fuel to carry autonomous cars to success. There will be legal roadblocks that stretch for metaphorical miles, computer crashes that are worse than 100 car pile ups, battles over regulations longer than the Harry Potter series, and untold glitches from retooling the roads, our homes and our cities. But those won't get in the way of the ease of tapping your fingers on a smartphone and watching Jeeves roll around the corner just a few minutes later.

Thanks

Thanks to everyone who helped with this book, in particular:

- Alex Dominguez—Editing

- Caroline Wayner—Editing

- Richard Johnson—Editing

- Will Rodger—Editorial Guidance

- David Whitcomb—Editorial Guidance

- Levon Kazarian—Editorial Guidance

- Henry Fountain—Editorial Guidance

- Kirsty Pargeter—Cover illustration
  (see `kjpargeterimages.co.uk`)

Finally, the bibliography does not contain URLs to save space. They're available on request.
-Peter Wayner
Baltimore, MD
April 2015
p3@wayner.org

Bibliography

[1] National Highway Traffic Safety Administration. Traffic safety facts. (DOT HS 811 161), 2008.

[2] National Highway Traffic Safety Administration. Traffic safety facts, 2010 data. *NHTSA*, (DOT HS 811 630), June 2012.

[3] Ron Amadeo. California DMV says Googles autonomous car tests need a steering wheel– state isn't ready to approve Google's cars without a backup control system. *Ars Technica*, August 21 2014.

[4] Warren H. Anderson. *Vanishing Roadside America*. University of Arizona Press, 1981.

[5] Arbitron. Arbitron national in-car study: 2009 edition. 2009.

[6] Dan Aykroyd, Harold Ramis, and Rick Moranis. *Ghostbusters*. Black Rhino Productions, Columbia Pictures Corporation, and Delphi Films, June 8 1984.

[7] Emily Badger. Taxi medallions have been the best investment in america for years. now Uber may be changing that. *Washington Post*, page 1, Nov 27 2014.

[8] Lisa Balde and Anthony Ponce. Woman gives birth in cicero traffic jam roads were blocked for nearby fatal car fire, police said. *NBC-Chicago*, January 23 2013.

[9] Radley Balko. How municipalities in St. Louis County, Mo., profit from poverty. *Washington Post*, September 3 2014.

[10] H. Ballon and Museum of the City of New York. *The Greatest Grid: The Master Plan of Manhattan, 1811-2011*. Columbia University Press. Museum of the City of New York, 2012.

[11] Alastair Barr. A Google car without a steering wheel? not so fast, California says. *Wall Street Journal*, August 21 2014.

231

[12] Josh Barro. Under pressure from Uber, taxi medallion prices are plummeting. *New York Times*, page A1, Nov 27 2014.

[13] Lousi Bedigain. Amazon's lockers coming to Staples. *Forbes*, November 7 2012.

[14] Michael Biesecker. Outer Banks evacuating ahead of Irene. *Salisbury Post*, August 25 2011.

[15] Mark Binelli. How Detroit became the world capital of staring at abandoned old buildings. *New York Times*, November 9 2012.

[16] George Orwell (Eric Blair). *1984*. Houghton Mifflin Harcourt, 1983.

[17] Terry Box. Consumers already thinking about things they can do in autonomous cars. *Dallas Morning News*, February 14 2015.

[18] Bettine Boxall. New storm water runoff rules could cost cities billions. *Los Angeles Times*, November 9 2012.

[19] J. Brouws. *Roadside America: 30 Postcards*. Chronicle Books LLC, 2003.

[20] Genevieve Shaw Brown. Ryanair will fly to the US for $14, CEO says. *ABC News*, February 27 2014.

[21] Nicholas Burress. Looking into the new grid— a review of Tron: Legacy. *Yahoo Voices*, Jan 13 2011.

[22] David Byrne, Brian Eno, Christopher Franz, Jerry Harrison, and Tina Weymouth. Once in a lifetime. *Remain in Light*, February 2 1981.

[23] Steven A. Camarota and Karen Zeigler. Jobs americans wont do? a detailed look at immigrant employment by occupation. *Center for Immigration Studies*, August 2009.

[24] Nicholas Carlson. Uber warns customers New Year's Eve pricing 'is not for the faint of heart'. *Business Insider*, December 30 2012.

[25] Ralph Carmichael, Paul Hampton, Allan Burns, and Chris Hayward. *My Mother the Car*. Cottage Industries Inc. and United Artists Television, September 14 1965.

[26] AJ Carothers. The sunday drive. *My Three Sons*, 1(35), June 1 1961.

[27] Rod Chadwick. Harold Bate and his marvelous chicken-powered car. *Mother Earth News*, (8), March 1971.

[28] C.C. Chan and K.T. Chau. *Modern Electric Vehicle Technology*. Monographs in Electrical and Electronic Engineering Series. Oxford University Press, 2001.

[29] Rebecca Chao. Massive Chinese holiday traffic jam: Tennis games break out on the road. *Ars Technica*, October 1 2012.

[30] Mary M. Chapman and Micheline Maynard. Fewer youths jump behind the wheel at 16. *New York Times*, February 25 2008.

[31] Chinacanuck. The cars that ate china (review). *imdb.com*, July 29 2008.

[32] Chris Christoff and Ian Kolet. American gun deaths to exceed traffic fataliteis by 2015. *Bloomberg*, December 19 2012.

[33] Nicola Clark. Wpuld Ryanair deal make economy class even more crowded? *New York Times*, September 8 2014.

[34] The Clash. Red angel dragnet. *Combat Rock*, May 14 1982.

[35] Stephanie Clifford. E-commerce, with bricks and mortar, too. *New York Times*, December 19 2012.

[36] coldwave171. Car insurance in france must be expensive ... (review of "ronin"). *imdb.com*, April 23 2003.

[37] Pullman Company. *Car service rules of the operating department of Pullman's palace car company, revised Sept. 1st, 1893*. W.H. Pottinger, printer, 1893.

[38] Larry Copeland. One in seven drivers have no insurance. *USA Today*, September 12 2011.

[39] Michael Corkery and Jessica Silver-Greenberg. Miss a payment? good luck moving that car. *New York Times*, September 24 2014.

[40] Alex Cox. *Repo Man*. Edge City, March 2 1984.

[41] Cameron Crowe. *Say Anything ...* Gracie Films and Twentieth Century Fox Film Corporation, April 14 1989.

[42] Les Crutchfield and John Meston. *Monopoly*. Gunsmoke, October 4 1958.

[43] Mary Cummings. The flying car will finally fly – and drive. *Scientifc American*, January 8 2013.

[44] Stephanie Darral. They don't make them like that any more! the 107-year-old car that's NEVER broken down. *Daily Mail*, August 29 2011.

[45] Larry David, Jerry Seinfeld, Majorie Gross, Jonathan Gross, Ron Hauge, Charlie Rubin, and Carol Leifer. *The Fusilli Jerry*, volume Season 6, Episode 20. Seinfeld, 1995.

[46] Alex Davies. An autonomous car is going cross-country for the first time. March 13 2015.

[47] G.G. Deák. *Picturing New York: The City from Its Beginnings to the Present*. Columbia University Press, 2000.

[48] dhuey. Singapore: any travelers been framed for drug smuggling? *Flyertalk.com*, February 5 2006.

[49] Clay Dillow. Radical ideas: By adding sensor arrays, postal trucks could become a nationwide data-collecting network. *Popular Science*, December 20 2010.

[50] Clay Dillow. Boston's 'street bump' app tries to automatically map potholes with accelerometers and GPS. *Popular Science*, February 10 2011.

[51] Ray Dippolito. *Handicapped*. Mariano Films, September 26 2008.

[52] K.C. Douglas and Robert Geddins. Mercury boogie. Later titled, "Mercury Blues" when recorded by Steve Miller Band (1976), David Lindley (1981), the Finn Pave Maijanen (1987), Alan Jackson (1993), Meat Loaf (2003) and Dwight Yoakam (2004)., September 1949.

[53] Peter Egan. Viva Terlingua! Shelby's supercharged v-6 Terlingua Mustang, driven to its namesake Texas ranch. *Road and Track*, July 8 2008.

[54] Les Emmerson. Signs. *Good-byes and Butterflies by Five Man Electrical Band*, 1970.

[55] EPA. Fy 2011 annual report underground storage tank program. *Environmental Protection Agency*, (EPA 510-R-12-001), March 2012.

[56] Charles Siegel et. al. Removing freeways– restoring cities. *Preservation Institute– www.preservenet.com*, 2007.

[57] everyone. Road movie. *Wikipedia*.

[58] Jack Ewing. Carmakers try to figure out the new generation. *New York Times*, September 28 2012.

[59] Hampton Fancher, David Webb Peoples, and Philip K. Dick. Bladerunner. *Ladd Company and Shaw Brothers and Warner Bros*, June 25 1982.

[60] Mike Farrell and Larry Gelbart. *The Yalu Brick Road*, volume 8. from M*A*S*H, November 19 1979.

[61] Katie Fehrenbacher. Tesla unveils free solar-powered car charging stations for Model S owners. *GigaOM*, September 24 2012.

[62] Will Ferrell and Adam McKay. *Talladega Nights: The Ballad of Ricky Bobby*. Columbia Pictures, Relativity Media, and Apatow Productions, August 4 2006.

[63] Helen Fields. Road rage: Can sitting in traffic trigger a heart attack. *U.S. News and World Report*, November 1 2004.

[64] Carmen Finestra, David McFadzean, Matt Williams, and Jon Vandergriff. When harry kept delores. *Home Improvement*, Includes "Mercury Blues" sung by Alan Jackson(Season 5, Episode 18), February 20 1996.

[65] Keith First. Removing traffic engineering control— the awkward truth? *Tecmagazine*, pages 73–79, February 2011.

[66] R.M. Fogelson. *Downtown: Its Rise and Fall, 1880-1950*. Yale UP, 2003.

[67] Center for Disease Control. National hospital ambulatory medical care survey: 2009 emergency department summary tables. *CDC.gov*, 2009.

[68] Centers for Disease Control and Prevention (CDC). *Behavioral Risk Factor Surveillance System Survey Data*. U.S. Department of Health and Human Services, Centers for Disease Control and Prevention, Atlanta, Georgia, 2004.

[69] Centers for Disease Control and Prevention. Pedestrian safety: Fact sheet. 2010.

[70] Insurance Institute for Highway Safety. Car size and weight are crucial! *Status Report*, 44(4), April 14 2009.

[71] Campaign for Tobacco-Free Kids. Broken promises to our children. *Campaing for Tobacco-Free Kids*, December 6 2012.

[72] Scott Frank, Don Roos, and John Grogan. *Marley & Me*. Fox 2000 Pictures, Regency Enterprises and Sunswept Entertainment, 2008.

[73] John Kander Fred Ebb. Theme from new york, new york. *Capitol*, June 21 1977.

[74] Al Friedman and Robert Swanson. The action. *Starsky and Hutch on ABC*, 3(13), January 7 1978.

[75] Ben Geier. Driverless cars could mean fewer cars on the road. *Fortune*, February 9 2015.

[76] Donna St. George. More teens are choosing to wait to get driver's license. *Washington Post*, January 24 2010.

[77] J. Ghonghadze. *Essays on Micromotives and Macrobehavior, Expectation Formation, and Asset Price Dynamics*. Schriftenreihe volkswirtschaftliche Forschungsergebnisse. Kovač, 2013.

[78] Martin Goldsmith and Martin Mooney. *Detour*. Producers Releasing Corporation (PRC), November 7 1945.

[79] Matt Gorening, David X. Cohen, and J. Stewart Burns. *Futurama: Where the Buggalo Roam*, volume 4. March 6 2002.

[80] Ken Greenberg. *Walking Home: The Life and Lessons of a City Builder*. McClelland & Stewart Limited, 2012.

[81] Daniel Gross. Has flying become more eco-friendly than driving? – it depends on the traveler. *Slate*, July 16 2014.

[82] J. Gunnell. *Weird Cars*. Krause, 1993.

[83] B. Hamper. *Rivethead: Tales from the Assembly Line*. Grand Central Publishing, 2008.

235

[84] Garrett Hardin. The Tragedy of the Commons. *Science*, 162(3859):1243–1248, December 1968.

[85] Jonathan Harr and Steven Zaillian. *A Civil Action*. Touchstone Pictures, Paramount Pictures and Wildwood Enterprises, January 8 1999.

[86] Mark Harris. FBI warns driverless cars could be used as 'lethal weapons'– internal report sees benefits for road safety, but warns that autonomy will create greater potential for criminal 'multitasking'. *The Guardian*, July 16 2014.

[87] Mark Harris. These are the secrets Google wanted to keep about its self-driving cars. *Quartz*, August 21 2014.

[88] Tony Hatch. Downtown. *Pye /Warner Brothers*, (5494), November 1964.

[89] Angela Haupt. How to control road rage. *U.S. News and World Report*, August 30 2012.

[90] Amy Heckerling. *Clueless*. Paramount Pictures, July 19 1995.

[91] H.M.A.C. Henderson. *The New Poetry - An Anthology*. 1917.

[92] W.J. Hennigan. Flying car aims to take wing in the commercial market. *Los Angeles Times*, April 19 2012.

[93] F. Herbert. *Dune*. Ace Science Fiction Series. Ace Books, 1999.

[94] H. Higgins. *The Grid Book*. MIT Press, 2009.

[95] Chelsea Hoffman. UPS package theft caught on camera in Las Vegas. *Case To Case (www.chelseahoffman.com)*, November 10 2012.

[96] W.D. Holman. ... and let's ban sport utilities in midtown. *New York Times*, February 6 2000.

[97] E. Homberger. *The Historical Atlas of New York City, Second Edition: A Visual Celebration of 400 Years of New York City's History*. A Henry Holt reference book. Henry Holt and Company, 2005.

[98] Charles Hugh-Smith. Growth = waste. *Of Two Minds*, 2014(09), September 22 2014.

[99] Joseph Husband. *The story of the Pullman car*. A.C. McClurg & Co., 1917.

[100] Jamie Hyneman and Adam Savage. Episode 80 - Big Rig Myths. *Mythbusters*, June 6 2007.

[101] Jamie Hyneman and Adam Savage. Episode 82: Snow special. *mythbustersresults.com*, June 20 2007.

[102] Jamie Hyneman and Adam Savage. Episode 108 blind driving. *mythbustersresults.com*, October 8 2008.

[103] Ashley Halsey III. Driverless vehicles? even in D.C. streets? an autonomous car takes a capital test run. *Washington Post*, August 25 2014.

[104] Neal Israel, Pat Proft, Paul Boorstin, and Sharon Boorstin. Moving violations. *SLM Production Group and Twentieth Century Fox Film Corporation*, April 19 1985.

[105] Honesty J. Trimet bus, max & Portland streetcar. *Yelp*, August 4 2012.

[106] Alan Jackson. Mercury blues. *Arista*, also sung by Steve Miller Band (1976), David Lindley (1981), the Finn Pave Maijanen (1987), Meat Loaf (2003) and Dwight Yoakam (2004)., September 1993.

[107] Jim Jacobs and Warren Casey. Grease. *Broadhurst Theater*, February 14 1972.

[108] J.A. Jakle and K.A. Sculle. *The Gas Station in America*. Creating the North American Landscape Series. Johns Hopkins University Press, 1994.

[109] J.A. Jakle and K.A. Sculle. *Remembering Roadside America: Preserving the Recent Past as Landscape and Place*. University of Tennessee Press, 2011.

[110] Zack Kanter. How ubers autonomous cars will destroy 10 million jobs and reshape the economy by 2025. *CBS SF*, January 27 2015.

[111] Zachary Karabell. (mis)leading indicators – why GDP and other leading economic numbers distort reality. *Foreign Affairs*, 93(2), March/April 2014.

[112] Nick Karner and Daniel McCabe. *The Pod*. 2010.

[113] Jacob Kastrenakes. Google is testing its autonomous cars in a 'Matrix-style' version of California: Asked the DMV whether computer simulations count toward testing. *The Verge.com*, August 21 2014.

[114] Troy Kennedy-Martin, Donna Powers, and Wayne Powers. *Italian Job*. Paramount Pictures and De Line Pictures, May 30 2003.

[115] Sara Kessler. Report potholes, graffiti and neighborhood problems with startup mobile app. *Mashable*, June 29 2011.

[116] Andy Kiersz. The states that love wine the most. *Business Insider*, March 6 2014.

[117] John King. 15 seconds that changes San Francisco: The sweeping makeover that tranformed the city began 15 years ago today with the Loma Prieta earthquake. *San Francisco Chronicle*, October 17 2004.

[118] Dick Kinney and Milt Schaffer. *Motor Mania*. Walt Disney Productions, June 30 1950.

[119] Sean Kinney and Ross H. Martin. *Rubbernecking*. Fender Bender Films (Summary by Astrid Devi), 2000.

[120] D. Kirby, K. Smith, and M. Wilkins. *The New Roadside America: The Modern Traveler's Guide to the Wild and Wonderful World of America's Tourist Attractions*. Simon & Schuster Australia, 1992.

[121] David Kravets. Americans' challenge to no-fly list gets day in court. *Wired*, May 7 2012.

[122] Derek Kreindler. It's not just a car – it's my first car. *The Truth About Cars*, April 16 2012.

[123] Kris Kristofferson and Fred Foster. Me and Bobby McGee. *Columbia*, January 11 1971.

[124] Steve LeBlanc. On December 31st, it's official: Boston's Big Dig will be done. *Washington Post*, December 26 2007.

[125] Jay Leno. Why everyone should drive an old car - article. *Jay Leno's Garage*, March 23 2010.

[126] Doron Levin. The truth about GM's marketing moves. *CNNMoney*, May 29 2012.

[127] Barry Levinson. *Tin Men*. Bandai Films, Silver Screen Partners III and Touchstone Pictures, 1987.

[128] Frank Loesser and Damon Runyon. *Guys and Dolls*. November 24 1950.

[129] Annie Lowrey. Your commute is killing you. *Slate*, May 26 2011.

[130] Frank Lupo, Stephen J. Cannell, and Stephen Katz. Road games. 3(18), February 5 1985.

[131] Robert Lustig. Sugar: The bitter truth. *UCSF Osher Center for Integrative Medicine*, May 26 2009.

[132] Leslie Macmillian. Detroit narrowly approves vast land sale. *New York Times*, December 11 2012.

[133] MADD. Drunk driving fatalities fall below 10,000. *MADD Blog*, December 10 2012.

[134] Michael Mann. *Heat*. Warner Bros., Regency Enterprises, Forward Pass, December 15 1995.

[135] Matt McFarland. How self-driving cars would benefit americans more than world peace. *Washington Post*, February 10 2015.

[136] Joni Mitchell. Big yellow taxi. *Ladies of the Canyon*, July 1970.

[137] Eric Moskowitz. 2011. *Boston Globe*, February 9.

[138] Jim Motavalli. What's a Twike? it's half-bike, half-electric car. *MNN.com*, August 29 2014.

[139] Chunka Mui. Fasten your seatbelts: Google's driverless car is worth trillions (part 1). *Forbes*, January 22 2013.

[140] Chunka Mui. Google's trillion-dollar driverless car– part 2: The ripple effects. *Forbes*, January 24 2013.

[141] Anna Mukai and Yuki Hagiwara. Toyota retakes global lead from GM on disaster recovery. *bw*, January 28 2013.

[142] Grace Murano. 12 funniest 'no parking' signs. September 9 2010.

[143] NACSOnline. US convenience store count. *NACSOnline*, January 31 2012.

[144] O. Nash. *Verses from 1929 on*. The Modern library of the world's best books. Modern Library, 1959.

[145] Hal Needham, Robert L. Levy, James Lee Barrett, Charles Shyer, and Alan Mandel. *Smokey and the Bandit*. Universal Pictures, Rastar Pictures and Pat Hustis Camera Cars, May 27 1977.

[146] A. Niffenegger. *The Time Traveller's Wife*. A Harvest Book, 2003.

[147] Chris Oakes. Our ad on your car: $400 a month. *Wired*, April 24 2000.

[148] Anahad O'Connor. Teenage driving laws may just delay deadly crashes. *New York Times*, September 14 2011.

[149] Steve O'Donnell and Dan O'Keefe. The pothole. *Seinfeld*, (816), February 20 1997.

[150] Department of Commerce. The automotive industry in the United States. *SelectUSA*, September 24 2014.

[151] Department of Transportation (US). National highway traffic safety administration (nhtsa). traffic safety facts 2010: Pedestrians. 2012.

[152] Department of Transportation (US). Bicyclists and other cyclists. DOT HS 811 743, April 2013.

[153] Kevin Ohannessian. Autonomous cars may change our lives in unexpected ways. *Popular Science*, October 23 2014.

[154] Barry Orlando. Is the death of general aviation 'plane' to see? *Barry's Flying Blog*, May 20 2011.

[155] Akweli Parker. Does stop-start technology wear engines down? *Discovery Channel*, undated.

[156] Robotic Parking. Robotic parking systems increase revenue. *(Company sales literature)*, 2012.

[157] Robert Pear. Federal power to intercept messages is extended. *New York Times*, December 28 2012.

[158] David Pelcyger. Building a natural gas fleet? infrastructure not included. *PBS.org*, August 9 2012.

[159] Annette Peters, Stephanie von Klot, Margit Heier, Ines Trentinaglia, All-mut Hrmann, H. Erich Wichmann, and Hannelore Lwel. Exposure to traffic and the onset of myocardial infarction. *New England Journal of Medicine*, 351(17):1721–1730, 2004.

[160] Matthew Phenix. Hands off with Heathrow's autonomous pod cars. *BBC.co.uk*, September 10 2014.

[161] Matthew Philips. Does destroying highways solve urban traffic congestion? *Freakonomics.com*, May 13 2011.

[162] Jr Pierre de Saint Phalle. Flying cars hit market in 2012. *PBS Newshour*, May 30 2012.

[163] L. Pointer. *In Search of Butch Cassidy*. University of Oklahoma Press, 1988.

[164] Joe Pollicino. Amazon lockers hit 7-Elevens in Washington DC, let you grab a parcel with a Slurpee. *Engadget*, June 25 2012.

[165] Bill Prady, Richard Rosenstock, Steven Molaro, and Daley Haggar. The killer robot instability. *The Big Bang Theory*, 2(12), January 12 2009.

[166] Associated Press. Obama signs renewal of foreign surveillance law. *Associated Press*, December 30 2012.

[167] PrincessKsMom. Staying awake while driving all night? *disboards.com*, February 20 2009.

[168] Weimer Pursell. When you ride alone you ride with Hitler! *Printed by the Government Printing Office for the Office of Price Administration NARA Still Picture Branch*, (NWDNS-188-PP-42), 1943.

[169] Harold Ramis, Douglas Kenney, and Chris Miller. *Animal House*. Universal Pictures and Oregon Film Factory and Stage III Productions, July 28 1978.

[170] Jonathan Ramsey. Sony Pictures aquires a comedy about autonomous cars. *Autoblog*, Feb 22 2015.

[171] Mike Ramsey. Self-driving cars could cut down on accidents, study says. *Wall Street Journal*, March 5 2015.

[172] Kamala Rao. Seoul tears down an urban highway and the city can breathe again. *Grist: A Beacon in the Smog*, April 5 2011.

[173] Earl Mac Rauch and Mardik Martin. New york, new york. *Chartoff-Winkler Productions and Distributed by United Artists*, Directed by Martin Scorsese and Produced by Robert Chartoff and Irwin Winkler, June 21 1977.

[174] Michael Ravnitzky. The postman always pings twice. *New York Times*, page A23, December 18 2010.

[175] Steve Read. Difference between guns, cars and booze. *Denver Post*, May 1 2010.

[176] Richard Reed. No you can't drive better than an autonomous car. *the Car Connection*, August 1 2014.

[177] Reuters. Elderly drivers no more dangerous than 20-somethings: study. *Reuters*, August 23 2012.

[178] Emma Reynolds. Sky's the limit: World's first flying car on the market at 800,000 (and it's been in the air since 1946). *Daily Beast*, March 17 2012.

[179] Bruce Robinson. *Withnail & I*. Cannon Group and Cineplex-Odeon Films and HandMade Films, June 19 1987.

[180] Richard Rodgers and Oscar Hammerstein II. The surrey with the fringe on top. *Oklahoma*, March 31 1943.

[181] Damon Rose. Blind drivers at the steering wheel. *bbc*, April 14 2013.

[182] Anneli Rufus. 40 drunkest cities. *Daily Beast*, December 29 2010.

[183] Anneli Rufus. Who drinks the most alcohol. *Daily Beast*, December 29 2010.

[184] Joe Sachs and Michael Crichton. *A Long, Strange Trip*, volume 15. ER, February 5 2009.

[185] Michael Sallah and Robert OHarrow Jr. Police intelligence targets cash:reports on drivers, training by firm fueled law enforcement aggressiveness. *Washington Post*, September 7 2014.

[186] Michael Sallah, Robert OHarrow Jr., and Steven Rich. Stop and seize:aggressive police take hundreds of millions of dollars from motorists not charged with crimes. *Washington Post*, September 6 2014.

[187] J.P. Sartre. *No Exit and Three Other Plays*. Vintage International. Knopf Doubleday Publishing Group, 1976.

[188] Antonin Scalia. United States, Petitioner, v. Antoine Jones. *Supreme Court of the United States*, (10-1259), January 23 2012.

[189] Julia Scheeres. Judge to hear Air ID challenge. *Wired*, January 18 2003.

[190] Max Scheinin. *Tomorrow Never Dies (1997) – Grade B+*. IMDB.com, 1997.

[191] T.C. Schelling. *The Strategy of Conflict*. Harvard University Press, 1980.

[192] T.C. Schelling. *Micromotives and Macrobehavior*. W. W. Norton, 2006.

[193] Thomas Schelling. An astonishing sixty years: The legacy of Hiroshima. *he Royal Swedish Academy of Sciences, Stockholm*, December 8 2005.

[194] Ted Schillinger. *Evacuate Earth*. Atlas Media and Creative Audio Post, December 2 2012.

[195] Brandon Schoettle and Michael Sivak. Potential impact of self-driving vehicles on household vehicle demand and usage. *University of Michigan Transportation Research Institute.*, (UMTRI-2015-3), February 11 2015.

[196] Brandon Schoettle and Michael Sivak. Road safety with self-driving vehicles: General limitations and road sharing with conventional vehicles. *University of Michigan Transportation Research Institute.*, (UMTRI-2015-2), January 2015.

[197] Paul Schrader. Taxi driver. " *Columbia Pictures Corporation and Bill/Phillips and Italo/Judeo Productions*, February 8 1976.

[198] Stuart Schwartzapfel. Futuristic pod car combines gm vision, segway practicality. *Wired*, March 24 2010.

[199] Christopher Seward. UPS worker arrested in theft after Fedex delivery. *Ars Technica*, December 21 2012.

[200] Semil Shah. Uber's New Year's Eve surcharges demonstrate the harsh reality of dynamic pricing. *Tech Crunch*, January 1 2012.

[201] Aideen Sheehan. Flights to us will cost just 10€on Ryanair O'Leary. *Irish News*, February 26 2014.

[202] Theodore Shrady. What you may not know about George Pullman. *trainweb.org*.

[203] Dennis Shryack, Michael Blodgett, Dennis Shryack, Daniel Petrie Jr., Jim Cash, and Jack Epps Jr. *Turner and Hooch*. Touchstone Pictures and Silver Screen Partners IV, July 28 1989.

[204] Charles Siegel. Removing urban freeways. *Planetizen*, March 19 2007.

[205] Ryan Singel. Secret ID law to get hearing. *Wired*, December 7 2005.

[206] Ryan Singel. The great no-ID airport challenge. *Wired*, June 9 2006.

[207] Ryan Singel. Supreme court asked to rule on secret law. *Wired*, November 11 2006.

[208] Ryan Singel. Supremes won't hear secret law challenge. *Wired*, January 8 2007.

[209] Ryan Singel. US airport screeners are watching what you read. *Wired*, September 20 2007.

[210] Skyline. High yield parking concept for prime real estate locations. *(Company sales literature)*, 2012.

[211] Jeremy Smerd. All hail king cab! *Crain's New York*, June 17 2012.

[212] Jay Sommers, Dick Chevillat, Howard Merrill, and Stan Dreben. *Green Acres: The Rains Came*. Filmways Television, May 18 1966.

[213] Aaron Sorkin. *A Few Good Men*. Castle Rock Entertainment and Columbia Pictures Corporation, December 11 1992.

[214] Statemaster.com. Binge drinkers (most recent) by state. *Business Insider*, March 6 2014.

[215] Michael Butler (story, screenplay), Dennis Shryack (story, screenplay), and Lane Slate (screenplay). *The Car*. imdb.com and Universal Pictures (Summary based on imdb version by Claudio Carvalho), May 13 1977.

[216] Ronald Sullivan. Paramedics will use carts to skirt traffic. *New York Times*, June 28 1986.

[217] Ed Sykes. Charlottesville considers stormwater runoff fee. *NBC29.com*, September 24 2012.

[218] Sabrina Tavernise. States cut antismoking outlays despite record tobacco revenue. *New York Times*, December 6 2012.

[219] Chap Taylor, Chap Taylor, and Michael Tolkin. *Changing Lanes*. Paramount Pictures and Scott Rudin Productions, April 12 2002.

[220] Craig Timberg. Web-connected cars bring privacy concerns. *Washington Post*, March 5 2013.

[221] Michael Todd. Commuting to an early grave. *Popular Science*, April 12 2013.

[222] Neil Tolkin. *License to Drive*. Twentieth Century Fox Film Corporation and Davis Entertainment, July 6 1988.

[223] Jason Torchinsky. Mercedes self-driving car seems to have gone rogue in san francisco. March 4 2015.

[224] Phill Tromans. Are you ready for autonomous vehicles? *The National*, August 28 2014.

[225] Chris Turner. The best tool for fixing city traffic problems? a wrecking ball. *Mother Nature Network (mnn.com)*, April 15 2011.

[226] uncredited. The university of michigan is building a fake city for driverless cars. *CityMetric*, August 5 2014.

[227] David Undercoffler. Ces 2015: Mercedes-benz shows off self-driving car of the future. *Los Angeles Times*, January 5 2015.

[228] unsigned. *Hot Rod*. IMdB (summary by Les Adams), October 22 1950.

[229] unsigned. Lethal weapon 4. *ScreenIt.com*, 1998.

[230] unsigned. Shifting gears: The in-car study. *Arbitrong and Edison Media Research*, 2003.

[231] unsigned. King of the jungle. *Classic Driver*, December 14 2005.

[232] unsigned. Tourists start evacuating North Carolina outer banks ahead of Hurricane Earl. *TimesHerald-Record Online*, July 10 2010.

[233] unsigned. Intelligent street lighting saves up to 80% on energy. *Science Daily*, July 13 2011.

[234] unsigned. Michigan is pothole paradise. *Detroit News*, March 14 2011.

[235] unsigned. Nissan and Nichicon to launch the "LEAF to home" power supply system with "EV power station". *Nissan Press Release*, May 30 2012.

[236] unsigned. Tesla unveils faster electric car charging station. *Associated Press*, September 25 2012.

[237] unsigned. Oregon officials propose per-mile tax for gas sippers. *Associated Press*, January 2 2013.

[238] unsigned. Hurricane information. *Outer Banks Beach Guide*, August 2014.

[239] S. Van Rensselaer and M.G. Van Rensselaer. *History of the City of New York in the Seventeenth Century*. Number v. 1. Cosimo, Incorporated, 2013.

[240] Matthew L Wald. In two-way charging, electric cars begin to earn money from the grid. *New York Times*, page B3, April 25 2013.

[241] Gy Waldron and Fred Freiberger. Route 7-11. 1(12), May 4 1979.

[242] Victoria Ward. Queen's chauffeur suspended as as buckingham palace security is exposed. *Mirror*, May 25 2009.

[243] Jonathan Watts. Gridlock is a way of life for Chinese. *The Guardian*, August 24 2010.

[244] Company Website. Mobilizing civic engagement. *www.citysourced.com*, 2012.

[245] Larry Webster and staff. Most fun for $25,000. *Car and Driver*, October 2008.

[246] Richard Webster. 6-year-old girl steals and wrecks mom's BMW driving to dad's house. *Examiner.Com*, February 4 2013.

[247] Matthew Weiner. *Smoke Gets In Your Eyes*, volume 1. Mad Men, 2007.

[248] J. Welsh, B. Howes, and K.J. Holland. *The Cars of Pullman*. Mbi Publishing Company, 2010.

[249] Yvonne Wenter. Parking violations bring in $13.5m for Baltimore City. *Baltimore Sun*, December 21 2013.

[250] Billy Wilder, Samuel A. Taylor, and Ernest Lehman. Sabrina. *Paramount Pictures*, 1954.

[251] Brian Wilson and Michael Love. Fun, fun, fun. *The Beach Boys*, February 3 1964.

[252] T. Wolfe. *The Right Stuff*. Picador, 2008.

[253] T. Wolfe. *The Kandy-Kolored Tangerine-Flake Streamline Baby*. Picador, 2009.

[254] Queenie Wong. Bill may recoup lost gas tax revenue. *Oregon Statesman Journal*, January 2 2013.

[255] Erica Wygonik and Anne Goodchild. Evaluating co_2 emissions, cost, and service quality trade-offs in an urban delivery system case study. *IATSS Research*, 35(1):7 – 15, 2011.

[256] Thirteen/WNET New York. Taxi dreams. *PBS.org*, 2001.

[257] David Zax. Using your car to power your house? another node in the smart grid. but it wont come cheap. *Technology Review*, June 12 2012.

[258] Robert Zemeckis and Bob Gale. *Back to the Future*. Universal Pictures, Amblin Entertainment, and U-Drive Productions, July 3 1985.

[259] Robert Zemeckis and Bob Gale. *Back to the Future Part II*. Universal Pictures and Amblin Entertainment and U-Drive Productions, November 22 1989.

[260] Kim Zetter. Man banned mid-trip by No-Fly list gets stranded in Hawai'i. *Wired*, October 22 2012.

[261] Benjamin Zhang. This study revealed the staggering potential of self-driving cars. *Business Insider*, June 2 2014.

www.ingramcontent.com/pod-product-compliance
Lightning Source LLC
Chambersburg PA
CBHW051859170526
45168CB00001B/171